D1314260

Stirring Up a World of Fun

International Recipes, Wacky Facts & Family Time Ideas

NANETTE GOINGS

new
hope
PUBLISHERS
Birmingham, Alabama

New Hope® Publishers
P. O. Box 12065
Birmingham, AL 35202-2065

Library of Congress Cataloging-in-Publication Data

Goings, Nanette.
  Stirring up a world of fun : international recipes, wacky facts &
family time ideas / Nanette Goings.
      p. cm.
  Includes index.
  ISBN-13: 978-1-56309-919-9 (soft cover)
  ISBN-10: 1-56309-919-5 (soft cover)
  1. Cookery, International. 2. Christian life. I. Title.
  TX725.A1G473 2006
  641.59--dc22

                        2006006790

ISBN-10: 1-56309-919-5
ISBN-13: 978-1-56309-919-9
N064138•0606•4M1

Contents ▪▪▪▪▪▪▪

Introduction ....

"So the people went away to eat and drink at a festive meal, to share gifts of food, and to celebrate with great joy because they had heard God's words and understood them" (Nehemiah 8:12 NLT).

Stirring Up a World of Fun: International Recipes, Wacky Facts & Family Time Activities offers families at home and Christian educators in church settings the opportunity to sample food from other countries, to learn about new cultures, and to discover how God's Word may be applied in their lives.

Each of the recipes, a gastronomic journey to faraway places, include a "Did You Know?" section, which gives a fact about the recipe's originating country or a wacky fact about one of the recipe's ingredients. The "What Can You Do?" portion provides a fun family-time or Christian education activity to help the recipe bring God's Word into the experience. And finally, the "What Does the Bible Say?" segment provides a Bible verse that can be learned, applied, and memorized during the week.

Be sure to look for symbols indicating recipes:

for children to make

that require adult assistance

that should be made by experienced adult cooks

Kitchen Safety Tips

Before you begin cooking, keep the following guidelines in mind:

- Always wash your hands before handling food items.
- Always pull back long hair and roll up sleeves.
- Always gather ingredients in the recipe before beginning to cook.
- Wash all fruits and vegetables thoroughly before cutting them.
- Use a clean, damp cloth to wipe all surfaces you'll be using. Keep the damp cloth handy while cooking to wipe up any spills that may occur.

- Always use hot pads to handle anything hot, and ask for adult assistance, if needed.
- Never leave cooking food unattended, and turn off all appliances when finished.
- Use caution when cutting with sharp knives on a cutting board.
- Measure carefully. Use nested cups in different sizes for measuring dry ingredients, such as flour and sugar, and a liquid measuring cup with lines drawn on the side to tell you how much liquid you have.
- Involve everyone in the cleanup.
- Remember, foods from different cultures may have unfamiliar tastes. Begin by sampling each food, taking small portions; this also discourages waste.

Experience God's world and Word as your tasty tour begins!

Stirring Up a World of Fun in a World of Fun in Africa

Egypt	Kenya	Namibia	Tanzania
The Gambia	Madagascar	Senegal	Togo
Guinea	Mali	Sierra Leone	Zimbabwe

Egypt........

Kousherie (Lentils with Rice and Noodles)

½ pound brown lentils
Salt water
¼ pound spaghetti
Water
3 cups cooked rice

3 large onions
2 tablespoons butter or
   margarine
Tomato sauce (optional)
Yogurt (optional)

Cook lentils in boiling salt water until tender (about 1 hour). Drain. Break spaghetti into 2-inch pieces. Cook in boiling water until tender. Drain. Peel and slice onions. Sauté onions in butter or margarine until brown (some Egyptians like them crispy black). Mix together the lentils, rice, and spaghetti.

Did You Know?

A *shabti* is a little figurine that can be found in ancient tombs in Egypt. This figurine is said to help the dead man with his farming chores in the afterlife. Today, you can buy these little figurines in Egypt, but be careful! Some figurines may look very old, but they really aren't. Some street vendors encourage their geese to swallow the small figurines. When a shabti reappears several days later, it looks very old, allowing a vendor to call it an Egyptian relic.

What Can You Do?

Many people in Egypt have not heard of Jesus' resurrection or His death on the Cross. Glue two craft sticks together to form a cross. Place a magnet strip on the back of the cross. Spread glue on the front surface of the cross. Sprinkle on top of the glue Egyptian spices of coriander seeds, cumin seeds, sesame seeds, and dried mint leaves (all found in the spice section of your grocery store). Let glue dry, and then place the cross magnet somewhere where you will see and smell it often. Each time you smell the wonderful spices, remember to say a prayer for people in Egypt who do not know Jesus.

What Does the Bible Say?

"The earnest prayer of a righteous person has great power and wonderful results" (James 5:16 NLT).

The Gambia ....

Sweet Peanut-Flavored Rice

1 cup cooked rice
2 tablespoons peanut butter
2 teaspoons sugar
⅓ cup milk

Put the cooked rice, hot or cold, into a bowl. Put 2 tablespoons peanut butter on top of the rice. Add 2 teaspoons of sugar. Pour ⅓ cup milk on top and stir until all of the ingredients are mixed together.

Note: *Many children are allergic to peanuts. If you are using this book in a group setting, check with parents before serving.*

Did You Know?

The national sport of the Republic of Gambia is wrestling. Before each wrestling match begins, each wrestler brings his own drumming group to draw attention to the match and get the crowd excited. Each ethnic group has its own special drumming tunes to play for their wrestler. During the wrestling match, the wrestler who remains standing the longest is the winner. When the winner is declared, supporters rush into the arena and press coins into his hands.

What Can You Do?

As a family, talk about what it means to wrestle with God. You might even want to read the story of Jacob who wrestled with God in Genesis 32. Jacob physically wrestled with God, and he also wrestled with God in prayer. As you pray for the people of the Republic of Gambia, as well as for others who struggle in life, lock arms wrestler-style and pray that Jesus will fill their hearts.

What Does the Bible Say?

Jacob said, "I saw God face to face, and yet my life was spared" (Genesis 32:30 NIV).

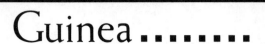

Guinea ....

Rice with Peanut Sauce

1 chicken, cut up
¼ cup oil
1 large onion, minced
4 tomatoes, chopped (or 3/4 cup tomato paste)

2 hot peppers (or 1 green pepper) chopped
1 cup ground peanuts (or peanut butter)
2 chicken bouillon cubes
Cooked rice

In large pot, cover chicken with water and boil for 1 hour. Drain, and set the broth aside. In a large, heavy skillet, heat the oil. Stir in onions, tomatoes, and peppers, and sauté until tender. Add peanuts (or peanut butter), bouillon cubes, chicken, and broth (just enough to create a sauce). Simmer until the oil rises to the top of the sauce. Serve over hot rice.

Note: *Many children are allergic to peanuts. If you are using this book in a group setting, check with parents before serving.*

Did You Know?

Guinea's capital of Conakry has 156 inches of rain a year, making it the wettest capital in the world! That's 13 feet of water—deeper than most swimming pools! The average high temperature, remember that's average, is 85°F and the average low temperature is 74°F. It's always a good idea to keep your mouth and eyes closed when going outside during the months of December through February in Guinea. When the strong harmattan winds blow in from the Sahara desert, the skies fill with gray sand.

What Can You Do?

Water is an integral aspect of the climate, environment, and lifestyle around the world. Today, have all family members count the number of times they use water. Remember to count each time you wash your hands, rinse off a piece of fruit, cook rice for dinner, or take a shower. At the end of the day, add up the totals from all family members and pray for that number of people in the Republic of Guinea, where only 1 percent of the people are Christian.

What Does the Bible Say?

"Rain and snow fall from the sky and don't return without watering the ground. . . . The same is true of the words I speak. They will not return to me empty" (Isaiah 55:10–11 NCV).

Stuffed Melon

1 large honeydew melon or cantaloupe or medium-sized watermelon

2 ripe papayas or mangoes

1 cup seedless grapes

2 tablespoons lemon juice

1 tablespoon orange juice

Slice off the top of the melon to use as a cover. Scoop out the melon. Remove seeds and cut up melon. Cut up papayas or mangoes. Mix melon with all other ingredients. Put fruit mixture back in melon shell and replace top. Keep refrigerated until ready to serve.

Did You Know?

Cantaloupe most likely originated in India and New Guinea. It received its name from the Italian word, *cantalupo*, meaning "wolf howl." Surely the wolf must have been howling because he knew all of the healthy benefits of eating cantaloupe. Cantaloupe, and melons in general, have been used to treat fevers, high blood pressure, arthritis, cancer, and skin diseases. And, when you've eaten your fill, slices may be applied to burns to aid healing or used as a facial to freshen your dry and tired skin.

What Can You Do?

After eating a healthy dinner, gather the family together and go on a brisk walk through the neighborhood to get your heart really pumping. If certain family members have short legs and can't keep up, push them in a stroller or let them ride their bikes, wearing safety helmets, while Mom and Dad set the pace! Take care of your body and feel better in the process by participating in one family heart-pumpin', body-healin' activity each day. When you arrive home, pray together thanking Jesus for healthy bodies.

What Does the Bible Say?

"Don't ever think that you are wise enough, but respect the LORD and stay away from evil. This will make you healthy, and you will feel strong" (Proverbs 3:7–8 CEV).

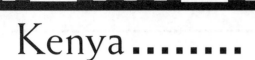

Kenya ....

Chicken Curry

4 large white onions, thinly
  sliced
½ cup oil
2 cinnamon sticks, broken in
  pieces
5 whole cloves
1 teaspoon turmeric
2 tablespoons curry powder

1 teaspoon cumin seeds
3 tomatoes, peeled
1 to 2 hot green chilies
1 thumb-sized piece fresh ginger
3 cloves garlic
2 tablespoons tomato paste
1 fryer chicken, cut up, skinned
Cooked rice

Sauté onions slowly in oil for about 20 minutes or until golden. Add cinnamon, cloves, turmeric, curry powder, and cumin seeds. Fry and stir over low heat about 5 minutes. Mix tomatoes, hot green chilies, ginger, and garlic together. Add to the onion mixture and cook for several minutes. Add the tomato paste and stir. Add chicken pieces. Cover and cook on low heat until chicken is very tender, about 1 hour. Stir occasionally. Serve over cooked rice. Pass condiments to put on top. Possible condiments: mango chutney, peanuts (roasted and hulled), chopped tomatoes, papayas, pineapples, oranges, grated fresh coconut, chopped green pepper, onions, boiled eggs, raisins.

Did You Know?

Female Kenyan boxer Conjestina Achieng was able to continue to work toward her dream of becoming a World International Boxing Federation champion, after receiving sponsorship from a Kenyan dairy and a voucher for four chickens a week for a year. The dairy sponsorship included a year's supply of milk and yogurt. The advancement of her career as a boxer had been at stake because of her dietary training needs and the shortage of food and poverty in her country.

What Can You Do?

Millions of families around the world face hunger and famine each day. If your family always has more than enough to eat, plan to set aside the money you would have spent on a dinner out and donate it to a local, national, or international hunger project. And, instead of eating until you are full, serve only food left over in the refrigerator from a previous dinner, or maybe left-over rice from the chicken curry for dinner some night. Hunger hurts! Pray for those who suffer each day.

What Does the Bible Say?

"Arise, . . . cry out in the night, at the beginning of the watches; pour out your heart like water before the face of the Lord. Lift up your hands toward Him for the lives of your young children, who faint from hunger at the head of every street" (Lamentations 2:19 AMP).

Madagascar ....

Salady Voankazo (Fruit Compote with Lychee Fruit)

1 cup fresh pineapple, cut into 1-inch pieces

1 cup cantaloupe, cut into small pieces

1 cup oranges, peeled and thinly sliced

½ cup canned lychee fruit (found in the Asian food aisle of the grocery store or in a specialty market)

½ cup sugar

¼ teaspoon salt

2 tablespoons lemon juice

2 tablespoons vanilla extract

Combine pineapple, cantaloupe, and oranges in bowl, and stir until well blended. Pour canned lychee fruit over the cut fruit. In a saucepan, bring sugar, salt, and lemon juice to a boil. Then boil for 1 minute. Remove syrup from heat. Stir in vanilla. Pour the hot syrup over the fruit. Put it in the refrigerator to chill for at least 1 hour.

Did You Know?

Madagascar, the fourth largest island in the world, sits off the east coast of Africa in the Indian Ocean. Lychee trees, which are grown in locations with tropical climates like Madagascar, were first brought to Hawaii in 1873. Reverend W. M. Brewster imported lychee trees to Florida in the early 1900s. Besides being yummy, lychee fruit also helps tame a cough!

What Can You Do?

Hunger and poverty are major issues in Madagascar. Tonight, before eating dinner, measure out 1 teaspoon of dried rice. After counting the grains of rice, multiply the total number by .7 to derive 70 percent—the number of people in Madagascar who go hungry each day. Pray together for those affected by hunger and poverty in the country of Madagascar.

What Does the Bible Say?

"All they asked was that we should continue to remember the poor, the very thing I was eager to do" (Galatians 2:10 NIV).

Mali . . . .

Jollof Rice

1 canned chicken, fully cooked
1 onion, chopped
1 (6-ounce) can tomato paste
2 cups uncooked rice

4½ cups water
Salt and pepper
1 package frozen mixed
vegetables

Drain chicken and cut up into large pieces. Place in a large pot. Add onion, tomato paste, rice, and water. Season with salt and pepper. Bring to a boil. Reduce heat to low and cook 10 to 15 minutes. Add mixed vegetables. Bring to a boil again, then reduce heat and cook over low heat until rice and vegetables are fully cooked.

Did You Know?

One of the biggest festivals in Mali is the Diafarabe Cattle Crossing festival. At this festival, the young women spend days getting ready to greet the young men returning from months of herding cattle in the desert. Two days are set aside prior to the boys' arrival for girls to braid their hair and another two days for them to weave coins and amber beads into their hair. Girls who have married since the festival the year before, usually wear the amber beads arranged in a circle around their head. Unmarried girls may also wear amber beads in their hair, but usually these are arranged in rows on their heads.

What Can You Do?

As a family, read 2 Samuel 14:25–26 and Judges 16:15–19 from the Bible. Talk about the role of hair in these two Bible stories. Contemplate and discuss the reasons God used something as ordinary as hair, to become the downfall of both of the men in these Bible stories. If possible, visit the Locks of Love Web site (http://www.locksoflove.org) and get information about the children who have benefited from this organization that provides hairpieces for those suffering from long-term medical hair loss. Discuss this information with your family. Pray for the children who seek help from Locks of Love. Maybe you can donate your own hair, if it is long enough.

What Does the Bible Say?

Your beauty should not come from outward adornment, such as braid ed hair and the wearing of gold jewelry and fine clothes. Instead, it should be that of your inner self, the unfading beauty of a gentle and quiet spirit, which is of great worth in God's sight" (1 Peter 3:3–4 NIV).

Namibia........

Sweet and Sour Braai [BRY] Sauce

1 cup tomato sauce or ketchup
1 teaspoon celery salt
1 cup water
1 teaspoon chili powder
5 tablespoons brown sugar
1 teaspoon salt

5 tablespoons vinegar
Dash pepper and hot pepper sauce
5 tablespoons Worcestershire sauce

Mix all ingredients and boil. Use the sauce like a barbeque sauce on meat. Baste meat during cooking and use remaining sauce as a dip for the meat.

Did You Know?

The annual Meatco Inter Boerebraai takes place in Namibia each spring. This nation-wide barbeque competition challenges serious grillers from around the country to prepare a full three-course meal, consisting of grilled hors d'oeuvres, bread, steak, and salad, to earn the top prize. Judges also challenge each team to utilize a surprise ingredient of the judges' choice in each of their entries. Previous year's champions have won a spring-bok (a kind of gazelle) hunt on a farm in southern Namibia, accompanied by a trained hunting guide, of course.

What Can You Do?

Host your own neighborhood Boerebraai this week. Encourage each family member to create his or her own menu of a "perfect" meal using the braai sauce from the recipe above. Encourage youngest family members to include a fruit or vegetable salad, a side dish, and a favorite kind of bread. The winning meal, decided by your family chef, may be a combination of all menus. Or invite neighborhood guests to vote for their favorite recipe.

What Does the Bible Say?

"The best thing we can do is to enjoy eating, drinking, and working. I believe these are God's gifts to us, and no one enjoys eating and living more than I do" (Ecclesiastes 2:24–25 CEV).

Senegal........

Chou (Beef Stew)

2 tablespoons oil
I pound beef cubes
3 large onions, diced
7 bouillon cubes
5 garlic cloves, crushed with a
    little water
I small can tomato paste

4 cups hot water
Cabbage
Carrots
Eggplant
Okra
Pumpkin
Potatoes

Dissolve the bouillon cubes in water and add to the beef cubes, onions, and garlic cloves; then brown these ingredients in oil. Add tomato paste and water. Cut all vegetables in large chunks, and add to meat mixture. Cook until meat is done and vegetables are tender. Serve over rice.

Did You Know?

Who your parents are is important for members of the Senegalese Wolof tribe. This is the way a person's place in society is determined. Because of a system of ranking, families of warriors are deemed the most important, followed by families of farmers, then blacksmiths, and finally, *griots* [GREE-oh], the cultural historians. Even though the griots do not rank highly in Senegal's society, they are respected because they are in charge of passing on the family and village stories.

What Can You Do?

Enjoy a time of talking about some of your family's stories. Need some help in getting started? How about retelling a funny story about when your grandmother was a child? Do the children in your family know a story about when they were born? How about asking Mom to describe the church she went to when she was a child. Does Dad remember what his favorite Bible story was when he was a child? Family stories can be a gift to each generation that preserves them by remembering, retelling, and passing them on.

What Does the Bible Say?

"Love the Lord your God with all your heart, all your soul, and all your strength. Always remember these commands I give you today. Teach them to your children, and talk about them when you sit at home and walk along the road, when you lie down and when you get up" (Deuteronomy 6:5–7 NCV).

AFRICA

Sierra Leone ....

Ata (Hush Puppies)

2 (1-pound) cans black-eyed
   peas
1 onion, minced

Cayenne pepper or hot pepper
   sauce
Salt to taste
Oil

Drain peas well and mash in a blender. Place in bowl and stir until fluffy. Slowly add warm water, beating constantly until the mixture is light and fluffy and drops easily from a spoon. Add minced onion, cayenne, and salt to taste. Heat oil, drop mixture by spoonfuls, and fry until brown.

Did You Know?

The name of each village, town, or city in the world is carefully chosen to reflect its location or something in its past. Even though Chicago is the third largest city in the US and a leading economic center, it got its name from Native Americans who named it for the wild onions that grew in the marshland. In Sierra Leone, village names are just as unique.

The town of Kumala, a Koranko word meaning "a person who talks too much," is named for the man who first settled the town. Bo is a town named for its generosity. When an elephant was killed close to the town, people came from surrounding villages to receive their portions. Hunters in the village of Bo spent days distributing the meat and saying, "*Bo-lor*," "This is yours."

What Can You Do?

As a family, work together to discover the meaning of the names we use each day. Using dictionaries, the Internet, baby name books, grandparents' recollections, or any other research tools, delve into what your first and last names mean. Research the meaning of the name of the town in which you live. Do a little research to find out why your street is named as it is. Then, open your Bible and use Bible commentaries to research the meaning of some of the names of people in the Bible.

What Does the Bible Say?

"God said to him, 'Your name is Jacob, but you will no longer be called Jacob; your name will be Israel.' So he named him Israel" (Genesis 35:10 NIV).

Tanzania ....

Mandazi (Corn Doughnuts)

I cup cornmeal	**I egg**
½ cup white flour	**Milk**
2 teaspoons sugar	**Oil**

Sift dry ingredients into a bowl. Beat egg and stir gently into dry ingredients. Add enough milk to give dough a dropping consistency. Pour enough oil into a heavy pan to barely cover the doughnuts. Heat the oil until it is bubbling hot, then gently drop a spoonful of mixture into the oil. Turn the doughnut over and over until it is golden brown. Take cooked doughnuts out of the oil and place on layers of paper towels to absorb excess oil. Serve hot.

Variations:

1. Try using white flour instead of cornmeal.
2. Try using honey or syrup instead of sugar; it should be added to the liquid mixture.

Did You Know?

Tingatinga is a Tanzanian term for a form of art originally created in the 1960s by artist Eduardo Saidi Tingatinga. This art form is created by using bicycle paint on Masonite (a form of fiber board). Vines, designs, and patterns fill in the empty space around the central item such as an animal. Tingatinga is sometimes called "airport art," because the finished paintings are never too large to be transported home on an airplane.

What Can You Do?

Host your very own family Tingatinga art show. After dinner, cover the table; put on paint shirts; set out paintbrushes, paints, and watercolor paper; and let the creativity begin! If you are feeling especially creative, dissolve one package of unsweetened fruit-flavored drink mix in 1/2 cup water for each color of scented "paint" you would like to use (this paint will stain). Use cotton swabs, chenille stems, fingers, or grape stems in place of paintbrushes. Remember, a true Tingatinga painting begins with a central item; then all the spaces around the focal image are filled in with vines, shapes, and designs. When the paintings are dry, create an art show and display the paintings for family and friends to admire. After viewing the exhibit, go outside to view the night skies and enjoy the "paintings" God has created!

What Does the Bible Say?

"The heavens tell about the glory of God. The skies show that his hands created them" (Psalm 19:1 NIrV).

Togo ....

Petepete or Piti-Piti (Mashed Potatoes)

2 pounds potatoes
I cup oil
I (8-ounce) can tomato puree
I (16-ounce) can tomatoes
I medium onion, chopped

Spices to taste: thyme, basil,
**   rosemary, oregano**
2 beef bouillon cubes
Salt to taste

Cook potatoes in lightly salted water until done but not mushy. In the meantime, make an African sauce by heating the oil and adding in the tomato puree and canned tomatoes that have been pureed in the blender. Continue cooking and stirring the sauce. Add onion, spices, beef bouillon cubes, and salt. Cook the sauce until thickened, then pour over the cooked potatoes. Stir well. (There is no liquid. It's like mashed potatoes.) Eggs, fish, or meat may be cooked and added to the sauce.

Did You Know?

Even in the twenty-first century, child trafficking can be big business in some West African countries. Child traffickers lure children from their homes with the promise of good schooling, career training, and pay to support their families at home. Young Togolese children report that they could not afford to pay their school fees, so they agreed to work in Nigeria harvesting crops, selling bread, and cleaning houses to get money for school or to give to their families. However, after working several months up to two years, many of the children ran away from the oppressive work without any pay or were sent away with only a bicycle for payment.

What Can You Do?

Talk about chores each family member does in your home. Are they jobs that benefit the family throughout the week? Do these jobs lessen the workload for Mom or Dad? Maybe the jobs benefit the child, such as making a bed or setting the table. Discuss the epidemic of child trafficking in some countries around the world. Encourage the children in your family to write a prayer for these abused and forgotten children, and remember to pray for them each night before going to bed.

What Does the Bible Say?

"I assure you, unless you turn from your sins and become as little children, you will never get into the Kingdom of Heaven. Therefore, anyone who becomes as humble as this little child is the greatest in the Kingdom of Heaven" (Matthew 18:3–4 NLT).

Zimbabwe ....

Fat Fry Recipe

2 cups self-rising flour
Pinch of salt
1 egg
1 tablespoon sugar
1 cup water

Mix ingredients well. Heat oil on a stove. Drop tablespoons of the batter into the hot oil. Cook until golden brown.

Did You Know?

You probably have eaten sausage for breakfast, but did you know that sausage also grows on trees? The countryside in Zimbabwe is covered with sausage trees. The sausage-shaped brown fruits on these trees grow up to three feet in length, seven inches in diameter, and can weigh more than 20 pounds. The sausage fruits make tasty meals for monkeys and elephants, and local residents grind the fruits into a paste to use as a blemish cream. This special cream is becoming known worldwide as a possible treatment for skin cancer.

What Can You Do?

Take a walk in your neighborhood looking for trees with interesting fruits, pods, cones, or seeds. Only after asking permission, collect a sample of any unfamiliar pods or fruits you see. Using your local library or the Internet, discover more about the trees in your neighborhood. Talk at dinner about your collected treasures and the information you have gathered. Pray for the neighbors you met while on your walk, and make a point of going back to visit those neighbors to share the tree information you have learned.

What Does the Bible Say?

"Jesus said, 'Remain in me, and I will remain in you. No branch can bear fruit by itself; it must remain in the vine. Neither can you bear fruit unless you remain in me'" (John 15:4 NIV).

Stirring Up a World of Fun in Asia

China	Japan	Pakistan	Taiwan
Hong Kong	Macao	South Korea	Thailand
India	New Zealand	Sri Lanka	

China ....

Chow Mein Noodle Cookies

½ cup butterscotch chips   I cup chow mein noodles
¼ cup peanut butter   ½ cup miniature marshmallows

Melt the butterscotch chips and the peanut butter together in a bowl in the microwave for I minute. Gently stir in the noodles and the marshmallows. Drop by spoonfuls onto waxed paper and let sit until firm.

Note: *Many children are allergic to peanuts. If you are using this book in a group setting, check with parents before serving.*

Did You Know?

How about a cup of tea with your chow mein noodle cookies? Tea is still the most common drink in China. However, each year a popular soft drink is gaining in popularity. Some of the adults in China drink concoctions with an herb base consisting of lizards, bees, or pickled snakes. Another drink for adults, maotai, is made from sorghum, smells like rubbing alcohol, and can be used as paint thinner. Pour me another cup of tea, please!

What Can You Do?

Make some tasty hot lemon tea mix by combining 1 package of unsweetened lemon flavored drink mix with 1 cup powdered instant tea in a resealable quart-sized plastic bag. Seal the bag well and shake to combine the ingredients. When you serve your family a cup of hot lemon tea, dissolve 2 teaspoons of the mix in a mug of hot water. You may add sugar to taste, if you wish. As your family sips tea, pray for people in China who may need to hear about Jesus.

What Does the Bible Say?

"As a deer gets thirsty for streams of water, I truly am thirsty for you, my God" (Psalm 42:1 CEV).

Raindrop Soup

1 can sliced water chestnuts
2 green onions, sliced
3 cups of chicken broth
1 cup of cooked, diced chicken

Put all ingredients in a pan and bring to a boil. Then turn down the heat, cover the pan, and simmer for 15 minutes.

Did You Know?

Did you know Chinese bird's nest soup is made from the nests of the tiny swiftlet bird? The swiftlet lives in dark caves and makes its nest from strands of its own saliva, which becomes hard when exposed to the air. Some Asian families make their income by delicately prying the nests from cave walls, a dangerous occupation in which many people fall to their deaths each year. Once the nests are cleaned and sold to restaurants, they are simmered in chicken broth and the resulting soup is sold to customers who are willing to pay quite a hefty sum (as much as $60 per bowl) to taste this delicacy.

What Can You Do?

Encourage children to help Mom or Dad clean up your family's "nest." Sort through the clothes in your closet and the shoes under your bed, and decide which ones to donate to a local charity that distributes clothing to people in need. And, while you're checking under your bed for shoes and stray socks, how about vacuuming, dusting, and organizing that space? You'd hate to have any swiftlets make a nest under your bed!

What Does the Bible Say?

"When you give a gift to someone in need, don't shout about it as the hypocrites do. . . . But when you give to someone, don't tell your left hand what your right hand is doing" (Matthew 6:2–3 NLT).

Hong Kong........

Cashew Nut Chicken with Vegetables

2 pounds chicken breasts
1 tablespoon soy sauce
½ teaspoon sugar
½ teaspoon cornstarch
1 teaspoon grated ginger

1 (10-ounce) can button mushrooms
1 (8-ounce) can water chestnuts
1 (10-ounce) package frozen peas
½ to 1 cup unsalted cashews

Cut chicken into 1-inch pieces. Marinate in soy sauce, sugar, and cornstarch for 1 hour. Stir-fry ginger and chicken over medium heat. Add mushrooms, water chestnuts, and peas. Add cashew nuts, mix well, and serve hot.

Note: *Many children are allergic to nuts. If you are using this book in a group setting, check with parents before serving.*

Did You Know?

Endangered Chinese White Dolphins live along the coastline near the mouth of the Pearl River by Hong Kong. They are born almost black and change quickly to a light gray color, and then become white or pink. There are only about 120 of these unique dolphins in the Hong Kong area. They are thought to become pink, like flamingos, because of the pigment in food they eat—crabs and shellfish. These beautiful dolphins have become an endangered species because of water and air pollution, loss of habitat, and boat traffic.

What Can You Do?

Did you know that there are currently more than 24,000 species of animal that are endangered or threatened by human activities? Discuss ways in which your family may help these endangered populations and create a better environment for all of us to live in. Look around your home and come up with some specific ideas. To get you started thinking, consider cutting down on your usage of disposable plates and cups that end up in landfills, using organically friendly fertilizer on your lawn, carpooling to reduce air pollution, or using phosphate-free laundry and dish soaps.

What Does the Bible Say?

"So God created great sea creatures and every sort of fish and every kind of bird. And God saw that it was good. Then God blessed them, saying, 'Let the fish multiply and fill the oceans'" (Genesis 1:21–22 NLT).

Chinese Almond Cakes

¾ cup sugar
1 teaspoon baking powder
¼ teaspoon salt
¾ cup butter or margarine, softened

1 egg
2 tablespoons water
1 teaspoon almond extract
2½ cups plain flour
Whole almonds

Combine sugar, baking powder, salt, butter, egg, water, and almond extract. Mix with a mixer at medium speed for about 1 minute. Gradually add flour. Blend at low speed. Shape dough into 1-inch balls. Place on greased cookie sheet about 2 inches apart. Flatten balls slightly and press a whole almond firmly into the center of each cookie. Bake at 350°F for 8 to 12 minutes until firm but not brown (do not overbake). Immediately remove from cookie sheets.

Did You Know?

What happens in Hong Kong on Sunday that doesn't happen any other day of the week? All of the domestic help, people employed to clean and manage another person's home, get the day off! Thousands of Indonesian, Filapina, Nepalese, and Thai maids meet in the streets, beaches, and parks to spend the day with their friends. However, since nationalities almost never mix, there are specified areas for each ethnic group to congregate.

What Can You Do?

Who does most of the cleaning at your house? Is it Mom or Dad, Grandma or Big Sister? How about giving that family member some time off from their normal chores? One evening have the children take charge of cleaning up after supper. Include chores such as clearing off the table, loading the dishwasher, washing the pots and pans in the sink, and sweeping the floor. Remember to tell the people in your household who cook, clean, and make the home run efficiently that you appreciate what they do each day.

What Does the Bible Say?

"Whoever wants to be a leader among you must be your servant, and whoever wants to be first must become your slave. For even I, the Son of Man, came here not to be served but to serve others, and to give my life as a ransom for many" (Matthew 20:26–28 NLT).

Soy Lemon Chicken Wings

2 tablespoons oil
10 to 15 chicken wings (upper portion of the wings)
1 thinly sliced lemon

½ cup soy sauce
½ cup brown sugar
Water to cover

Pour the oil into a saucepan, and then layer in chicken wings and lemon slices. Pour in soy sauce, brown sugar, and water to cover all the layers. Cover the pan and cook on low or medium heat for 30 minutes or until done.

Did You Know?

The avian flu, which infects millions of chickens across Asia each year, has now become a threat to humans. This is quite an unusual event! Scientists think that the spreading of avian flu to humans has become possible because of poor sanitation in meat markets, the location of poultry farms to housing subdivisions, and poor hand-washing habits of those who work with chickens. Avian flu can also mutate into a greater health risk, which may then pass from human to human.

What Can You Do?

How many times do you touch your nose, mouth, or eyes during the day? Well, if you are average, you could answer approximately 200 times per day. And because germs can easily enter our bodies through our mouth, nose, and eyes, washing our hands often can be the only way to get rid of germs. As a family, practice washing your hands tonight before dinner with this teachable moment. Slather your hands with petroleum jelly as a reminder of those nasty, sticky germs. Try washing your hands with cold water, then try washing them with warm water. Finally, use soap and rinse with warm water. Discuss how washing with soap and water removes germs and helps to keep our bodies healthy. With clean hands, read Leviticus 15:11–12 together.

What Does the Bible Say?

"Young people can live a clean life by obeying your word"" (Psalm 119:9 CEV).

India.......

Chapatis (Flatbread)

2 cups whole wheat flour
⅔ cup warm water
2 teaspoons vegetable oil

Pinch of salt

Mix all of the ingredients in a large bowl, using a fork first, and then using your hands. Mix until you can make a ball. Knead the dough for about 10 minutes. Cover the bowl with a damp cloth and let the dough sit for 30 minutes. Roll the ball into a 12-inch log, and then cut it into 6 pieces. Use a rolling pin to roll each piece into a very thin circle, about 7 inches across, like a tortilla. Have an adult heat a cast-iron skillet on medium high. Place a chapati on the skillet, and cook it for 30 seconds. When the dough forms brown spots and bubbles, flip it with a spatula and cook it for 30 more seconds. Serve with chicken curry and rice. Use your chapati to scoop your food to your mouth!

Did You Know?

An Indian curry meal becomes the ultimate feast for the taste buds. Each Indian cook mixes her own unique blend of spices to create her own special curry powder that she adds to meat, fish, or vegetables. The rice, chapatis, and the mandatory condiments, called *sambals*, that make up a traditional Indian meal combine the flavors of sweet coconut or raisins, sour lemons, salty nuts, pungent pickles, tart apples, or yogurt to tingle and sooth the mouth when eating Indian food.

What Can You Do?

Pull out some of the spices in your kitchen and let family members enjoy the aromatic smells after dinner tonight. Some familiar herbs or spices may include sage, cinnamon, cloves, nutmeg, basil, oregano, garlic powder, vanilla, dill weed, and pepper. Discuss how the aroma of the spices remind you of a particular food or a special family event. Say a prayer together, thanking God for food to eat and good memories to share. Also, pray for families in India and around the world who have never heard about Jesus.

What Does the Bible Say?

"On the first day of the week, very early in the morning, the women took the spices they had prepared and went to the tomb. They found the stone rolled away from the tomb, but when they entered, they did not find the body of the Lord Jesus" (Luke 24:1–3 NIV).

Kaju (Seasoned Cashew Nuts)

1½ tablespoons vegetable oil
2 cups cashew nuts, shelled and unsalted

1 teaspoon salt
Dash of cayenne pepper
Black pepper (optional)

Measure the oil and put it in the frying pan to heat for 30 seconds. Add the nuts and sauté them in the oil for 3 minutes, turning them over and over with the spatula. Remove the nuts and put them on sheets of paper towels to drain. Pat them with an extra towel to remove any other oil. In a mixing bowl, combine the salt and pepper. Put the nuts into the bowl. Toss them with a spoon or your hands until they are coated with the salt and pepper.

Did You Know?

Indian people have many different eating habits. Muslims don't eat pork. Hindus don't eat meat of any kind. Jains, a small group of Hindus, believe that all living things have souls . . . even bugs. Consequently, some people will not eat anything grown underground, like potatoes or carrots, because they fear an insect may accidentally be hurt or killed while pulling up the plant.

What Can You Do?

Go on an expedition to hunt for an anthill in your yard or neighborhood. Without stepping on the hill, or getting in the way of the ants, take some time to observe the ants working in their colony. Place pieces of a cashew or two (without the seasonings) near the hill. Will the ants carry the cashew pieces inside their hill? Isn't it amazing how our great and mighty God created something so small as the industrious ant?

What Does the Bible Say?

"Take a lesson from the ants, you lazybones. Learn from their ways and become wise! Though they have no prince or governor or ruler to make them work, they labor hard all summer gathering food for the winter" (Proverbs 6:6–8 NLT).

Japan ....

Chicken Teriyaki

½ cup soy sauce
1 teaspoon sugar
1 teaspoon sesame oil
½ teaspoon ginger
1 pound boneless chicken, cubed

1 bunch green onions, cut into pieces
1 green pepper, cut into large chunks

Mix soy sauce, sugar, sesame oil, and ginger. Marinate chicken in sauce for 30 minutes to 1 hour. Place chicken and vegetables on skewers and cook over broiler or outside grill.

Did You Know?

Words in a language often give us clues as to what a culture values. *Gaman suru* and *otonashii* are two words that have traditionally been qualities valued in Japanese women. *Gaman suru* means "to be patient, to tolerate, and to endure." *Otonashii* means "meek, gentle, quiet, and obedient." So maybe these words are useful when combined with the Japanese word *genki*, which is a way to describe highly energetic, lively, and friendly children.

What Can You Do?

Has today been one of those days in your home when a family member's attitude needs a little adjustment? Has there been a shortage of patience, tolerance, and endurance, and an abundance of highly energetic, lively, and spirited children? Write the word *attitude* down the side of the page. Work together to create an acrostic of ways family members can help or be kind to others. Make sure each letter in the word *attitude* identifies something that will improve each person's attitude and will be a kind and helpful response to others in the family. When you are finished creating your *attitude* acrostic, read Matthew 5:1–12 together with your highly energetic, lively, and spirited children.

What Does the Bible Say?

"Blessed are the merciful, for they will be shown mercy. Blessed are the pure in heart, for they will see God. Blessed are the peacemakers, for they will be called sons of God" (Matthew 5: 7–9 NIV).

Okonomi-Yaki (Vegetable Pancake)

2 cups flour
1 teaspoon baking powder
Salt
1 cup fish stock

2 large cabbage leaves
1 egg
4 ounces ground pork
Vegetable oil

Sauce and condiments to individual taste: Worcestershire sauce, soy sauce, mayonnaise, ketchup, mustard.

Sift flour, baking powder, and salt together into a large mixing bowl. Adding the fish stock a little at a time, mix flour swiftly until smooth. Do not over mix. Cover the bowl with plastic wrap and leave for 30 minutes (if left too long, batter will become sticky). Remove hard section of cabbage leaves and cut into thin strips. Add egg, ground meat, and cabbage to batter and mix lightly. Grease heated skillet. Pour in batter and flatten out with spatula. When bubbles begin to form and the edges begin to dry, turn over and fry the other side. Brush over pancake with a sauce or condiment of your choice. When pancake begins to give off an aroma, turn off heat.

Did You Know?

The Osaka Castle in Osaka, Japan, was built in 1583. Castles became quite common in Japan during this era because of continual wars and natural disasters. Japanese castles usually consisted of three rings of defense. The Japanese lords lived in the inner most ring, the servants lived in the outer ring of the castle, and the samurai warriors lived on the grounds outside the castle. The higher the rank of the samurai warrior, the closer he lived to the castle. Originally, castles in Japan were made of wood. As they were rebuilt over time, concrete became the building material of choice.

What Can You Do?

Do you live in an area prone to hurricanes, tornadoes, blizzards, or earthquakes? Prepare your own disaster supply kit to help keep you safe in the event of an emergency. As recommended by the United States Federal Emergency Management Agency (FEMA), fill a large plastic tub with essential items such as a change of clothes for each person, sturdy shoes, a coat, lots of bottled water, canned food, a first-aid kit, a can opener, and a flashlight. For more specific instructions, check out FEMA's family-friendly Web site (http://www.fema.gov/kids). Also, include a Bible in your disaster supply kit. It's the most important book you will need in the midst of a disaster.

What Does the Bible Say?

"God is bedrock under my feet, the castle in which I live, my rescuing knight. My God—the high crag where I run for dear life, hiding behind the boulders, safe in the granite hideout" (Psalm 18:2 The Message).

Macao ....

Congee (Sweet Rice)

3 cups of water
1 cup of rice
Sugar
Cinnamon

Raisins
Salt
Onions
Chopped bacon

Let water come to a boil. Add rice. Cook until rice is mushy. Many Chinese eat congee just like this, but sometimes they add other ingredients. Sugar, cinnamon, and raisins make a sweet congee; and salt, green onions, and bacon make a savory congee.

Did You Know?

After a farmer plants a grain of rice, it takes between 130 and 170 days before it is ready to harvest. It takes 1,300 gallons of water to produce 2 pounds of rice. Now, to put things into perspective, 150 days is more days than are in a season of the year. And, an average person in North America uses about 1,300 gallons of water each day; it is enough water to fill a small swimming pool and enough water to fill a fire pumper truck. Two pounds of rice would only provide one helping at dinner for a family of eight.

What Can You Do?

Local food banks are always in need of food staples such as rice, macaroni, cereal, canned fruits, and vegetables. Go grocery shopping as a family to purchase these basic food items for those in need in your community. Before taking the food into the food bank, pray together in the car that the food may nourish the bodies of the families who will receive it. Deliver the purchased food together as a family.

What Does the Bible Say?

"For God is the one who gives seed to the farmer and then bread to eat. In the same way, he will give you many opportunities to do good, and he will produce a great harvest of generosity in you" (2 Corinthians 9:10 NLT).

Gummy Raindrops

½ cup cranberry or apple juice
2 envelopes unflavored gelatin
2 tablespoons sugar

Pour the fruit juice into a saucepan, and heat over medium until it boils. Immediately sprinkle the gelatin over the juice and stir until gelatin dissolves. Cover a cookie sheet with waxed paper. Spoon the mixture in 1-inch drops onto the sheet. Allow the drops to cool slightly; then sprinkle lightly with sugar. Wait 10 minutes, then peel and eat.

Did You Know?

In Macao, the Moon Festival is celebrated in September or October, depending on the lunar calendar. It is a festive time for making lunar cakes for family and friends. Making lunar cakes requires muscles and stamina, as the ingredients must be energetically shaken until they are thoroughly mixed. Gazing at the new moon and leaving behind colorful lanterns at midnight for the gods of many religions are also traditions of the Moon Festival.

What Can You Do?

Create your own Light of the World Lantern from an empty glass jar or vase. With close adult supervision, have family members decorate the outside of the jar or vase with paint, Christian symbol stickers, and stars. Place a tea light candle inside the jar to remind you of Jesus, the Light of the world. Again, with close adult supervision, light the candle and turn out the lights in the room. Discuss how the candle lights up the dark room, then pray for people around the world who do not know Jesus. Before going to bed, blow out the candle and sing together, "Jesus Loves the Little Children" or "He's Got the Whole World in His Hands."

What Does the Bible Say?

"The Light shines in the darkness, and the darkness has not overpowered it" (*John* 1:5 *NCV*).

New Zealand ....

Frozen Chocolate Bananas

4 bananas
8 wooden craft sticks
I cup chopped nuts
I cup (8 ounces) chocolate chips

Peel bananas and cut them in half. Place each half on a stick. Freeze the bananas for a half hour to chill. Place a piece of waxed paper on a plate. Place chopped nuts on a paper plate. Put chocolate chips in a microwave-safe bowl and melt in the microwave. Remove bananas from the freezer and dip them in melted chocolate. Roll bananas in chopped nuts. Place on waxed paper, then place in the freezer for at least I hour.

Did You Know?

In 2003, the Tennessee Ugly Necklace Contest had one entry that used the often underappreciated banana peel. Participants interpreted ugly in different ways. Some of the contestants used materials they considered ugly—banana peels, being one. Other items strung to create a necklace were matted dog hair, rusty nails, and llama droppings. Besides being ugly, the rotting banana peel strung on the necklace felt icky on the skin. The winner of the contest received a $992.93 shopping spree at a beading supply store.

What Can You Do?

Recycling can become a great family activity. Go for a walk tonight around your neighborhood, in a park, at the nearest playground, or along a deserted road. Remember to take several large garbage bags with you, and wear rubber gloves when picking up trash. Designate one of the bags as a recycle bag. While you are picking up trash, place the recyclable items in the designated bag and take them to a recycling center or drop-off point close to you. You can probably consider any banana peels you might find as trash—unless you want to make a necklace!

What Does the Bible Say?

The heavens belong to the Lord, but he has given the earth to all humanity" (Psalm 115:16 NLT).

Pakistan . . . .

Chai (Tea)

2 tea bags   **½ cup milk**
⅔ cup water   **2 teaspoons sugar**

Put tea bags in boiling water and let the water boil for 5 minutes. Remove the tea bags. Pour in milk and sugar. Heat until it boils again.

Did You Know?

Pakistan is one of the highest per capita consumers of tea in Asia. However, poor growing conditions, a shortage of tea manufacturing plants, and a shortage of tea investors force Pakistan to rely mostly on imported tea from countries such as Kenya and Bangladesh. Pakistanis go to great extremes for a good cup of tea. In years past, 10 to 15 percent of the tea consumed in Pakistan was smuggled across the borders.

What Can You Do?

Save the tea bags used to make Chai. While they are still wet, gently blot and rub them on a piece of heavy cardstock. When saturated, place the paper between paper towels with a heavy book on top to assure the paper dries flat. The tea will make the cardstock look old. The next evening, after the paper has dried and while your family is together, talk about your house rules. Write the rules on the aged paper with a fine-tipped permanent maker to create your Family Constitution. Post the house rules in a prominent place.

What Does the Bible Say?

"Do you make the rules, or does God? You have to decide—I can't do it for you; now make up your mind" (*Job 34:33 CEV*).

South Korea........

Vegetable Pancake

1 large zucchini, coarsely grated
2 carrots, coarsely grated
1 large onion, finely chopped
1 clove garlic
2 eggs, lightly beaten
¼ cup water
1 tablespoon soy sauce

½ teaspoon salt
¾ cup flour
¼ cup vegetable oil

Sauce:
¼ cup soy sauce
¼ cup wine vinegar
1 tablespoon sugar

Mix vegetables in a medium mixing bowl; blend thoroughly. In a second bowl, beat together the eggs, water, soy sauce, and salt and blend thoroughly; then gradually fold in the flour until the mixture forms a smooth batter. Stir in the vegetable mixture until well blended. Heat the oil in a large frying pan. When it is hot, carefully arrange the mixture in the pan in heaping tablespoon-fuls; fry gently until they are browned on one side. Carefully turn over and fry until the pancakes are golden brown on the other side. Remove from the oil; drain on paper towels. To make the sauce, combine all the ingredients in a dipping bowl. Serve the pancakes at once with the sauce.

Did You Know?

Every August, the state of Vermont holds a zucchini festival. The big event of the festival is the Zukapult contest. Zuke lovers young and old create zucchini launchers to throw the Vermont state vegetable further than any other contestant. Zukapult rules require each entrant to supply 5 zucchini as ammunition for the armory. Each zucchini must weigh at least 8 ounces and no more than 32 ounces. Entrants select their ammunition from the armory based on a random draw. The current long distance Zukapult record is 150 feet.

What Can You Do?

Is there a picky eater who won't eat vegetables in your house? After dinner, read chapter 1 from the Book of Daniel in the Bible. Then slice some vegetables. Dip a slice of vege-table in fabric or tempera paint; gently press the painted side of the vegetable on a piece of construction paper or a piece of fabric. Use these veggie prints as place mats or as a tablecloth when they are dry.

What Does the Bible Say?

"So Daniel said to the guard, "For the next ten days, let us have only vegetables and water at mealtime. When the ten days are up, compare how we look with the other young men, and decide what to do with us" (Daniel 1:11–13 CEV).

Sri Lanka........

Gowa Mallung (Cabbage with Coconut)

½ pound brown lentils
Salt water
¼ pound spaghetti
Water
3 cups cooked rice

3 large onions
2 tablespoons butter or
  margarine
Tomato sauce (optional)
Yogurt (optional)

Wash and shred the cabbage, then place in a pan. Chop onion and pepper and add to the cabbage. Add salt and water and cook for 5 minutes. Stir; then add the coconut, pepper, and turmeric and cook for 2 to 3 minutes more. Sprinkle with lime juice just before serving.

Did You Know?

Coir, the fiber of coconut husks, is an important source of income for 40,000 Sri Lankans, mostly women. Soaked in water and then peeled from the husks of the coconuts, these fibers are spun into strands used for making rope, twine, doormats, brooms, and brushes. Small pools of water surrounded by dirt walls, called coir pits, are filled with pieces of coconut husks and allowed to soak until they are soft, sometimes taking several months. Workers stand up to their necks in the coir pits searching for husks that are pliable enough to spin. Spinning the coir into strands requires three people: one to turn the spinning wheel, two to walk slowly away from it, pulling the coir strands tight before twisting them into rope.

What Can You Do?

The tsunami of December 26, 2004, filled the lagoons of Sri Lanka with powerful rushing water, debris, and devastation. Thousands of people lost their homes, jobs, and family members. For each member of your family, cut a piece of twine long enough to wear as a bracelet. Wear the twine as a reminder of those Sri Lankan citizens affected by the tsunami. Talk about families you know who have recently lost their homes, jobs, or family members. Pray for them too. Throughout the week, each time you notice the twine on your wrist or feel its roughness against your skin, say another silent prayer for those mentioned.

What Does the Bible Say?

"He will not crush those who are weak, or quench the smallest hope, until he brings full justice with his final victory. And his name will be the hope of all the world" (Matthew 12:20–21 NLT).

Taiwan ....

Eight Precious Glutinous Rice Pudding

1 cup uncooked glutinous rice
½ cup sugar
2 tablespoons butter
2 tablespoons each of candied lotus seeds, melon peel, tangerine peel, fresh chestnuts, melon seeds. Other candied fruit may be used, such as raisins, dried persimmons, mango, pineapple. The items should total 8.

Wash and clean rice thoroughly. Soak in hot water for 2 hours. Steam or boil until rice is soft. Add sugar and butter and mix well. Arrange candied fruit in a pretty pattern in the bottom of a greased pudding mold or heat-resistant glass bowl. Pack rice mixture on top of fruit, pressing firmly. Cover with parchment paper and steam for 30 to 45 minutes. Unmold onto serving plate. Serve hot.

Did You Know?

The Taiwanese legend of Sun-Moon Lake tells the story of a brave couple who confronted two dragons that stole the sun and the moon. Because of the bravery of DaJianGe and ShuiSheJie, the dragons were destroyed, and DaJianGe and ShuiSheJie transformed into mountains, standing guard over the dragons' bodies in the lake and the round sun and moon in the sky. Each year, the people of the town of Cao Zu, Taiwan, show their gratitude to the couple in this legend by dancing the Holding Ball dance. In this dance, villagers each throw a colorful ball into the air and then use a bamboo stick to hold it up, symbolizing the sun and the moon in the sky.

What Can You Do?

Conduct your own version of the Holding Ball dance in your backyard. Use a broom handle and a lightweight playground or beach ball. Try to balance the ball on the stick while moving in a slow and graceful dance. When everyone in the family has had an opportunity to dance, sit down together and talk about what it means to be brave. Name people you know who are brave. Why do you think they are brave? What are some areas in your life in which you need to be brave? Pray to Jesus, asking for His power and strength in your life. Thank Jesus for His bravery of dying on the Cross for each one of us.

What Does the Bible Say?

"I've commanded you to be strong and brave. Don't ever be afraid or discouraged! I am the LORD your God, and I will be there to help you wherever you go" (Joshua 1:9 CEV).

Thailand . . . .

Khao Phat (Fried Rice)

5 green onions
3 tablespoons butter
I (6-ounce) can tiny shrimp, cleaned
2 cups cooked rice
2 teaspoons ginger

½ teaspoon garlic powder
½ teaspoon ground cloves
I teaspoon salt
½ teaspoon pepper
2 tablespoons soy sauce
2 eggs

Cut the onions into small pieces. Melt butter in a large frying pan. Sauté the onions, turning them until they are golden. Add drained cooked shrimp. Cook for 2 more minutes. Add the cooked rice. Cook I minute more. Keep turning over and over until all sides are done. Add all other ingredients except eggs. Stir. Break eggs into a small bowl. Beat them with a fork. Pour over the mixture in frying pan. Continue to turn all ingredients for 30 seconds more.

Did You Know?

Thailand was greatly affected by the Indian Ocean tsunami of December 2004. Thousands of people lost their lives, their livelihoods, and their homes. More than 12,000 families lost at least one member in their family. Many tourists from other countries in Asia are worried about ghosts in the affected parts of the country and they refuse to visit these areas. This has hurt the tourist trade and has hindered rebuilding. Thai leaders have tried to calm these fears to draw tourists back to the area.

What Can You Do?

Is your family ready for an emergency? Practice a fire escape plan for each member of your family, making sure children know a meeting location away from your home in the event of a fire. Teach young children the importance of knowing their address and knowing how to call for help in an emergency. If your community has an emergency warning system, familiarize your children with those procedures.

What Does the Bible Say?

"Do you not know? Have you not heard? The Lord is the everlasting God, the Creator of the ends of the earth. He will not grow tired or weary, and his understanding no one can fathom. He gives strength to the weary and increases the power of the weak" (Isaiah 40:28–29 NIV).

Sticky Rice and Banana Treat

1 banana, sliced
Rice (instant rice or "sticky rice" from a local Asian food store)
Banana leaf

Form a ball of cooked rice around a slice of banana. Wrap rice ball in a banana leaf. Grill over hot coals. Enjoy.

Did You Know?

In Thailand when a mother calls the family to dinner she says, "Let's eat rice" instead of "Let's eat." In China, girls who don't want to eat their dinner are told that every grain of rice they leave in their bowl represents a pockmark on the face of their future husband. Also, in China, "Have you had your rice today?" is the way you say the common greeting, "How are you?" In India, rice is said to be perfectly cooked when it is like "two brothers"—close but not stuck together.

What Can You Do?

Growing rice in Thailand is big business. Growing Christians in Thailand is slow and hard work. Christianity was introduced to the Thai people in the sixteenth century. Today, only .5 percent of the people profess to be Christians. After dinner, read together Mark 4:13–20. Pray for missionaries who are sowing the seed of Christianity in Thailand.

What Does the Bible Say?

"Others, like seed sown on good soil, hear the word, accept it, and produce a crop—thirty, sixty or even a hundred times what was sown" (Mark 4:20 NIV).

Stirring Up a World of Fun in

a World of Fun in

CENTRAL AND EASTERN EUROPE

Bosnia	Greece	Russia
Croatia	Hungary	Slovenia
Czech Republic	Romania	

Bosnia ....

Palicenke (Chocolate Crepes)

3 cups flour
2 tablespoons sugar
1 teaspoon baking powder
1 teaspoon salt
4 cups of milk

4 eggs
1 teaspoon vanilla
Nutella® spread or chocolate
    frosting

Mix the first 4 ingredients in a bowl. Add the next 3 ingredients. Stir with a wire whisk until smooth. Heat a skillet over medium heat. Pour ¼ cup of batter into skillet. Let the batter cover the bottom of the pan. Cook until light brown, and then flip the crepe. When the other side is light brown, remove it from skillet and place it on plate. Repeat. Spread chocolate on each crepe and roll it up.

Did You Know?

On June 24, 1981, six teenagers from the small village of Medjugorje, Bosnia-Herzegovina, saw a vision believed to be Mary, the mother of Jesus. Her message, "I have come to tell the world that God exists. He is the fullness of life, and to enjoy this fullness and peace, you must return to God," is said to provide strength and comfort to the millions of tourists who now flock to this tiny village each year. Tourists are able to participate in Catholic Mass offered in ten different languages. In a war-torn country such as Bosnia, Medjugorje has become a perceived place of safety for millions of people.

What Can You Do?

Watch a portion of the television evening news together as a family. Then turn off the television and pray for those people affected by war, hunger, violence, and terror. Pray for soldiers fighting for freedom, leaders of countries at war, hostages in unknown locations, and families living in fear. Pray for Jesus' healing love to soften the hearts of people around the world involved in war. Pray for protection, peace, and an end to war.

What Does the Bible Say?

But you, Lord, tell them, "I will do something! The poor are mistreated and helpless people moan. I'll rescue all who suffer" (Psalm 12:5 CEV).

Croatia.......

Stuffed Green Peppers

6 green peppers

Stuffing:
  1 pound ground meat
  1 teaspoon salt
  1 small onion, chopped
  ¼ teaspoon pepper
  1 egg, slightly beaten
  ½ cup cooked rice
  ½ teaspoon garlic powder
  2 tablespoons parsley

Tomato sauce:
  1 (6-ounce) can tomato
    paste
  1 tablespoon flour
  ½ cup water
  1 teaspoon oil
  ½ teaspoon salt
  2 teaspoons paprika
  1 teaspoon sugar

Cut off the tops of the green peppers. Wash and remove all the seeds. After browning the meat, mix it with the remaining stuffing ingredients and fill the green peppers. Mix the tomato sauce ingredients together in a large saucepan or dutch oven and bring to a boil. Put in the stuffed green peppers and simmer over low heat for 2 hours. Serve with mashed potatoes or bread.

Did You Know?

There are three kinds of Dalmatians—a spotted breed of dog, a group of people who live along the Dalmatian coast of Croatia, and an extinct language formerly spoken by inhabitants of the Dalmatian coast. Dalmatian, the language, seemed to appear during the tenth century with an estimated 50,000 speakers. Dalmatian speakers lived in towns on the seashore of Croatia; each city developed its own language. The last known speaker of Dalmatian dialect, Tuone Udaina, was killed by a land mine in 1898.

What Can You Do?

Does anyone in your home speak another language? Even if you can say only a few words, try to say them with each other. Then, open your Bible and read Genesis 11:1–8 as a family. Talk about why the people were trying to build the tall tower. Since God created humans "in His image," what was wrong with the people trying to build a tower to get closer to God? Close in prayer. Ask God for guidance to hear and understand Him when He speaks to us.

What Does the Bible Say?

"The Lord said, 'If, as one people all having the same language, they have begun to do this, then nothing they plan to do will be impossible for them. Come, let Us go down there and confuse their language so that they will not understand one another's speech.' So the Lord scattered them from there over the face of the whole earth, and they stopped building the city" (Genesis 11:6–8 HCSB).

Czech Republic........

Docci Bojoi (Christmas Cookies)

1 cup sweet butter	4 egg whites
1½ cups sugar	¾ cup walnuts, finely ground
1 egg yolk	1 teaspoon lemon extract
½ teaspoon salt	1 cup blackberry jelly
2½ cups flour	1 cup chopped walnuts

Cream butter with ½ cup sugar; add egg yolk and salt. Sift flour; measure and stir into mixture. Pat dough into a thin layer in the bottom of a 10-by-15-inch cookie sheet. While gradually adding 1 cup sugar, beat egg whites until they form stiff peaks. Gently fold in the ground walnuts and flavoring; spread jelly over dough and swirl meringue over jelly. Sprinkle meringue with chopped walnuts. Bake at 350°F for 40 minutes. Cut into squares. Makes 3 dozen.

Did You Know?

During Holy Week in the United States, we anticipate on Palm Sunday, commemorate on Maundy Thursday, contemplate on Good Friday, and rejoice on Easter Sunday. People in the Czech Republic observe Ugly Wednesday. This is the day to remind people of Judas's betrayal of Jesus. This is a family day when students get the day off from school and parents get the day off from work. But, it is not just a fun day; it is also a workday. On this day, the family works together to take mattresses, couches, and rugs outside and beat them until every particle of dust is gone. They wash windows and change out their curtains. Then, when the inside is thoroughly cleaned, the family paints the outside of the house. All work must be finished by evening!

What Can You Do?

You knew it was coming after that last section! Organize a Never-Been-This-Clean-Before Day at your house. Make a list of jobs to be completed by each member of the family. Wash windows, dust bedrooms, vacuum the carpets, and scrub that bathroom. When everyone starts getting a little tired and grumpy, hold hands and pray together, giving thanks to God for a home to live in and a clean one at that. Give thanks for hands that willingly help and families who work together for a beautiful result. After you are finished, you might want to test out your bed with the clean sheets.

What Does the Bible Say?

"God, I love living with you; your house glows with your glory. When it's time for spring cleaning, don't sweep me out with the quacks and crooks" (Psalm 26:8–9 The Message).

Knedliky (Stuffed Plum Dumplings)

6 pitted dark sweet plums
1 cup mashed potatoes
1 cup flour
¾ cup bread crumbs

1 teaspoon salt
¾ cup sugar
3 teaspoons cinnamon
½ cup butter

For dough, combine potatoes, flour, ½ cup bread crumbs, and salt, and beat until the dough is smooth and elastic. Roll out the dough to ¼-inch thickness, and cut into 6 squares. Place one plum in each square. Sprinkle with ½ cup sugar and 2 teaspoons cinnamon. Wrap each plum separately in a dough square, covering each plum completely. Boil dumplings in water for 10 minutes or until they come to the surface. Melt the butter in a skillet. In another bowl, mix together the remaining sugar, cinnamon, and bread crumbs. Drop cooked dumplings in the melted butter, and then roll cooked dumplings in the crumb mixture until thoroughly covered.

Did You Know?

In the Czech Republic, every day of the year is someone's Jmeniny (name day). If your name is Alice, your special day to receive small presents of flowers or chocolate would be January 15. Josef would celebrate his name day on March 19. Veronika would celebrate on February 7. Every name in Czech is on the name day calendar. And, to be polite, if you decide to give flowers to someone on their Jmeniny, don't give them an even number. In the Czech Republic, people give an even numbers of flowers only for funerals.

What Can You Do?

Designate a name day for each member of your family in the coming week. Make the name day special in small ways for your sister by making her bed, doing one of her chores, or making her favorite dessert for dinner. Dad might appreciate sleeping a while longer on his name day, while family members wash the car or mow the lawn as a special treat.

What Does the Bible Say?

"God said to Moses: . . . 'For I know you well and you are special to me. I know you by name'" (Exodus 33:17 The Message).

Raised Dumplings

1 cake compressed yeast
¼ cup lukewarm water
2 teaspoons salt
2 eggs, beaten
¾ cup milk, scalded and cooled to lukewarm

4 cups sifted flour
5 slices bread
1 tablespoon butter
5 quarts boiling pork broth (or other broth)

Crumble yeast in lukewarm water. Add salt and beaten eggs to milk and combine with dissolved yeast. Sift flour; measure and add to milk mixture, beating thoroughly until dough is smooth and elastic. Spread bread with butter and toast lightly; cut into cubes and fold bread into dough. Place dough in greased bowl and set in a warm place to rise. When doubled in size, mold into balls about the size of a walnut. Let rise again until almost doubled in size. Drop gently in pork broth and cook about 30 minutes. Yield: 6 to 8 servings.

Did You Know?

Loutkové divadlo, Czech puppet theater, is considered the best in Europe and among the top worldwide. Since the seventeenth century, families of traveling puppeteers have entertained children, adults, and most recently, tourists. Puppeteering is big business in Czech Republic, with festivals and international competitions throughout the year. If you plan to attend a Czech puppet show, you'll want a front-row seat so you will be able to see the action since no performances are in English!

What Can You Do?

Create your own low-cost, family puppet show. Use hand puppets made out of old socks, or make finger puppets by drawing faces, hair, and even double chins, on the pads of your fingers with narrow-tipped markers. Use the back of a couch or chair to create a puppet stage. Small props could include sewing thimbles for hats, rubber bands for belts, jar lids for beds, and clothespins for crowd scenes. When developing your script, base story themes on a familiar Bible story, a humorous family event, or a never-heard-before-fresh-from-your-mind idea. And, who says that your performance has to be in English?

What Does the Bible Say?

"It is truly wonderful when relatives live together in peace. . . . It is like the dew from Mount Hermon, falling on Zion's mountains, where the LORD has promised to bless his people with life forevermore" (Psalm 133:1, 3 CEV).

Greece ....

Moussaka (Greek Casserole)

1 large eggplant	Dash of nutmeg
1 pound ground beef	½ teaspoon oregano
1 onion, chopped	1 tablespoon chopped parsley
1 clove garlic, minced	2 cups tomato sauce
Salt	⅓ cup tomato paste
Pepper	¾ cup grated cheese

Cut eggplant into ½-inch slices. Place slices on cookie sheet. Brush with melted butter. Sprinkle with salt and pepper. Broil 5 minutes. Repeat on other side. Brown ground beef, onion, garlic, and spices. Stir in tomato sauce and paste. In 9-by-9-inch baking dish, layer half of eggplant slices and half of meat mixture. Repeat. Sprinkle with cheese. Bake 40 minutes at 350°F.

Did You Know?

The Greek year seems filled with one festival after another. Gynaikratia, on January 8 of each year, commemorates the festival of role reversal in the villages of northern Greece. Women spend the day in the cafes and city social spots where the men usually meet each day. The men stay home, do housework, and take care of the children.

What Can You Do?

On a rainy Saturday, when the children are bored and the parents are tired of entertaining them, turn the tables and celebrate the Greek festival of Gynaikratia North American style. Parents can play with toys and read a good book while children clean the bathrooms and make lunch. End your "festival" by talking about the ways each family member serves others each day of the week. Tell each other how much these acts of service are appreciated.

What Does the Bible Say?

"Whoever wants to become great among you must be your servant, and whoever wants to be first must be your slave—just as the Son of Man did not come to be served, but to serve, and to give his life as a ransom for many" (Matthew 20:26–28 NIV).

Hungary ....

Cucumber Salad

3 cucumbers, peeled
½ cup white vinegar
I medium onion, sliced
2 teaspoons sugar
Salt

Pepper
3 tablespoons sour cream
Paprika

Slice cucumbers into a bowl. Salt well, stir in vinegar, and let stand in refrigerator for several hours or overnight. To keep cucumbers crisp, remove excess liquid by squeezing cucumber slices between your hands. Place in a serving bowl. Stir in onion, sugar, salt, and pepper to taste. Chill until serving. Just before serving, pour off excess liquid if necessary, stir in sour cream, and sprinkle with paprika.

Did You Know?

Laszlo Bíró, a Hungarian journalist, sculptor, and painter, invented the first ballpoint pen. The Bíró, much like ballpoint pens today, used fast drying printer's ink and a small ball bearing that suctioned the ink from a reservoir inside the pen onto the paper. Bíró first patented the pen in 1938. When Laszlo and his brother moved from Hungary to Argentina, he patented the pen again in Argentina. His patent was later sold to the British Royal Air Force during World War II to be used by their pilots because Bíró's ballpoint pen would not leak at high altitudes as fountain pens did. Today, Inventor's Day in Argentina is celebrated on Laszlo Bíró's birthday, September 19.

What Can You Do?

For dinner conversation, think of family or friends who are experiencing a difficult time. Many things can make a person lonely or sad—moving away from family and friends, experiencing health issues, or dealing with the death of a loved one. After dinner, take out a few handy-dandy ballpoint pens and some stationery and have each family member write a note or illustrate a card for the people mentioned at dinner. Tell the recipients of your notes that they are thought of, prayed for, and loved. You might even include a little trivia about Laszlo Bíró and his first ballpoint pen.

What Does the Bible Say?

"Live a life filled with love for others, following the example of Christ" (Ephesians 5:2 NLT).

Paprika Chicken

1 large onion, chopped	Salt and pepper to taste
Vegetable oil	1 chicken, cut up
2 tablespoons sweet paprika	1 cup sour cream

In a large heavy pot, sauté onion in a small amount of vegetable oil until tender. Remove from heat and stir in paprika to coat onions. Salt and pepper chicken pieces, dredge in flour, and place in pot. Cook the chicken over medium heat until tender, adding a little water if necessary to keep moisture in pot. When finished, remove chicken pieces and set aside. Add a small amount of water to the pot and stir in sour cream to make thin gravy. Replace chicken and heat to serve. Serve with hot egg noodles or rice.

Did You Know?

Grown on the hot, southern plains of Hungary with an average of 2,000 hours of sunshine a year, Hungarian paprika is considered the most flavorful paprika in the world. The Hungarian pimento, shaped like a chili pepper, is grown and cultivated in small family plots. When the growing season has ended, the older women of the community gather together and string the harvested peppers using long needles and strands of twine. The women take their garlands of peppers home and hang them up to dry for several weeks. Once dried, they are grated. Hungarian paprika comes in at least seven shades, from a deep blood-red to a pale orange-red and varies accordingly in its intensity and flavor.

What Can You Do?

Before eating your Hungarian paprika chicken, mix together in a small dish, ½ teaspoon of paprika and 1 tablespoon of warm water. With a pen, draw the outline of a cross on a piece of cardstock. Use the paprika mixture to paint the dark wood of the cross. When the paprika paint is dry, write your own prayer on the back of the cardstock, thanking Jesus for His saving sacrifice on the Cross and for forgiving our sins. After saying your prayers, read together John 20:24–29 from the Bible.

What Does the Bible Say?

"Because you have seen me, you have believed; blessed are those who have not seen and yet have believed" (*John* 20:29 *NIV*).

Romania ....

Mamaliga (Cornmeal Grits)

I quart water
I tablespoon salt

I box yellow cornmeal

Put the water and salt in a heavy soup pot; bring to a boil. Pour cornmeal into your hand and let it sift slowly through your fingers into the boiling water, stirring constantly with a large heavy wooden spoon. Continue adding cornmeal until you get the desired thickness. Be careful to lower the flame when adding the cornmeal as it begins to boil again (there is a tendency for the cornmeal to bubble up suddenly, and you may burn yourself). Continue to heat and stir until the mush is very smooth. Then cover the pot and let cook slowly for 10 to 12 minutes longer. Turn out the mush onto a wooden board. Cut into slices and serve with meat stews, soups, milk, etc.

Did You Know?

The Voronet Monastery in Bucovina, Romania, is one of five monasteries that contain beautiful fresco paintings on the outside walls as well as the inside of the buildings. The anonymously painted frescoes of the Family Tree of Jesus and the Last Judgment were finished in 1535. The monastery was built by Saint Stephen the Great to fulfill a promise to his advisor, Saint Daniel the Hermit, who is buried in the monastery . . . except for his right index finger, which was encased in silver and buried in another Romanian monastery.

What Can You Do?

When was the last time you painted with finger paints? Purchase some freezer paper and finger paints, or make your own finger paints by mixing together 2 tablespoons of sugar and ⅓ cup of cornstarch in a saucepan. Slowly add 2 cups of cold water. Cook over low heat for 5 minutes, stirring until the mixture is a clear, smooth gel. When the mixture is cool, stir in ¼ cup of liquid dishwashing soap. Divide into portions and color with food coloring or powdered tempera. Create your own Family Tree of Jesus or the Last Judgment paintings. Remember to use only your right index finger for creating these beautiful works of art!

What Does the Bible Say?

"So come on, let's leave the preschool fingerpainting exercises on Christ and get on with the grand work of art. Grow up in Christ. The basic foundational truths are in place: turning your back on 'salvation by self-help' and turning in trust toward God" (Hebrews 6:1 The Message).

Vinete (Eggplant Spread/Dip)

3 large eggplants
I cup lemon juice
4 cloves garlic, minced

I small onion, grated
Salt to taste
¼ cup olive oil

Burn whole unpeeled eggplants on an open-flame grill or broil in an oven until the skin is crisp and the flesh is soft. Peel as soon as they are cool enough to handle. Place peeled eggplants in a blender; add remaining ingredients and blend thoroughly. Adjust seasoning to taste, adding more salt or lemon. Serve with fresh bread or as a dip with fresh vegetables.

Did You Know?

Thomas Jefferson first brought eggplant, classified as a fruit, to the United States. Originally only white in color, eggplant acquired its name because it looked like eggs hanging from the bushy plant. Before the twentieth century, people in Europe believed eating eggplant caused madness, leprosy, cancer, and bad breath. Because of these superstitious reasons, eggplants were mostly decoration until the twentieth century.

What Can You Do?

As a family, talk about some superstitions that people believe today. Do you know an athlete who wears the same "lucky" socks for every game? Do you know someone who fears a black cat crossing his or her path? Superstitions that have passed down through the years include: an itchy nose means a person would have a quarrel with someone; putting on a shirt inside out caused bad luck for the rest of the day; sneezing three times before breakfast or picking up a pencil on the street were good luck. Can you think of other superstitions? What motivates people to believe in such superstitions? How can you respond to others when they talk about "good luck," "bad luck," or "being lucky"? How can Colossians 2:8 help you respond?

What Does the Bible Say?

"Watch out for people who try to dazzle you with big words and intellectual double-talk. They want to drag you off into endless arguments that never amount to anything. They spread their ideas through the empty traditions of human beings and the empty superstitions of spirit beings. But that's not the way of Christ" (Colossians 2:8 The Message).

Russia ....

Borscht (Cabbage Soup)

Beef soup bone
¼ head cabbage
I small carrot
I small potato
I small onion

I small beet, cooked
Salt to taste
I to 2 tablespoons tomato
  paste
Sour cream

Boil the soup bone in a pot of water. Remove bone and cut off meat into small pieces. Shred the cabbage, carrot, potato, onion, and beet. Mix together. Fry half of the shredded vegetable mixture and put the other half in the meat broth. Put the fried mixture in the broth. Add the meat to the broth. Add 2 tablespoons tomato paste and salt to taste. Bring to a boil and simmer until vegetables are cooked. Serve in a bowl with I teaspoon sour cream on top.

Did You Know?

Soup is the perfect food! Every culture has some variety of soup. In ancient times, doctors prescribed ingredients softened in a liquid broth for invalids. Travelers during the colonial period carried "pocket soup." They reconstituted the soup with water when they arrived at their destination. Canned soup, what we can buy at the grocery store today, first became available during the nineteenth century. Take out your soup pot; throw in some vegetables, herbs, meat, and water, and savor the simmering aroma and taste of a world-class favorite food!

What Can You Do?

Host a One-of-a-Kind Soup Party! Make invitations on the back of a canned soup labels for each of your family and friends. On the invitation, say that each person attending the One-of-a-Kind Soup Party needs to bring a can of vegetables and a can of soup with them when they come. Mail or deliver your invitations well in advance of the party. Several hours before guests arrive, simmer chicken or beef in water to create the soup stock. Cut meat into bite-sized pieces, and season the broth to taste. As guests arrive, drain the canned vegetables and pour into the meat stock. Collect the cans of soup that guests provided and donate them to a local soup kitchen or food pantry.

What Does the Bible Say?

"When you go out to dinner with an influential person, mind your manners: Don't gobble your food, don't talk with your mouth full" (Proverbs 23:1–2 The Message).

Slovenia ....

Punjrnr Paprike (Stuffed Peppers)

4 large green peppers
4 ounces mushrooms
6 tablespoons butter
I clove garlic, crushed
½ pound ground beef
2 tomatoes, peeled and chopped

Salt and pepper to taste
I bunch of parsley, chopped
I cup cooked rice
3 tablespoons ketchup
I egg
¼ cup oil

Clean green pepper by cutting around the stem and taking out the seeds, making little cups. Clean mushrooms, cut into pieces, and sauté in butter for 5 minutes. Add garlic, tomatoes, salt, pepper, parsley, cooked rice, and ketchup. Cook until thoroughly heated. In a large bowl, combine ground meat and slightly beaten egg; mix well. Combine the warmed ingredients and the ground meat mixture. Sit peppers in a large cake pan or casserole dish, and stuff the peppers with the ground meat mixture. Cover with aluminum foil, and bake at 325°F for I hour.

Did You Know?

The Kravji Bal (Cow's Ball) held each mid-September in Bohinj, Slovenia, is an important date on the Slovenian dairy farmer's calendar. This day celebrates the return of the cows from their summer grazing in the high mountain pastures to their winter months in the valley. People set up booths to sell anything from alpine hats to wool slippers to wooden hay rakes. Other festival activities include traditional dancing and yodeling, followed by a parade of the herdsmen and their families leading garlanded cattle through the town and into the valley.

What Can You Do?

Before going to bed tonight, pour a glass of milk for each family member. Add some chocolate syrup and stir. While slowly sipping chocolate milk, discuss some of the following questions: What is your favorite snack? If you could make a favorite meal for our family tomorrow, what would you make? What word would you like to create to be in the dictionary . . . and what does it mean? If you invited Jesus over to our house, what do you think He would like to do with you?

What Does the Bible Say?

"For I said to your ancestors when I brought them out of slavery in Egypt, 'If you obey me and do whatever I command you, then you will be my people, and I will be your God.' I said this so I could keep my promise to your ancestors to give you a land flowing with milk and honey—the land you live in today. Then I replied, 'So be it, LORD!'" (Jeremiah 11:4–5 NLT).

Stirring Up a World of Fun in

THE MIDDLE EAST

Cyprus

Israel

Jordan

Lebanon

United Arab

Emirates

Cyprus ....

Meatballs in Egg and Lemon Broth

1 pound very lean ground meat (beef, lamb, pork, or a combination)
1 cup uncooked rice
3 eggs
Salt to taste

1 teaspoon mint or parsley, finely chopped
Flour
1 quart chicken stock or water with chicken bouillon cubes
1 lemon

Mix the meat, rice, and one egg together with the salt, chopped parsley, or mint and form into small balls. Roll these in flour. Meanwhile, bring the chicken broth or stock to a boil. Gently place the meatballs into the broth and simmer on a low for 15 to 20 minutes, or until rice is tender. Add water as necessary. There should be about 2 cups of broth when the meatballs are finished. Remove the meatballs to a warm serving dish. Prepare the egg sauce. Beat the remaining 2 eggs with the juice of the lemon and add a little of the hot broth to this mixture, beating continually. Stir the egg mixture back into hot stock. Do not boil, but heat until the mixture is thick. Pour the sauce over the meatballs, and serve with rice and a salad of mixed greens with oil and vinegar dressing.

Did You Know?

Friends of the Cyprus Donkey is a nonprofit, charitable association in Vouni Village, Cyprus. This group cares for old, sick, and unwanted donkeys from the island of Cyprus through sponsorships by people from around the world. Some donkeys have become too old to work or their owners have become too old to care for them. Or, when an owner dies, there is no friend or family member to take the donkey. Through this association, donkeys receive veterinary care and can live out the rest of their lives at the village.

What Can You Do?

Consider volunteering at the local animal shelter or offer to provide needed supplies. Contact the shelter to ask about their most urgent needs. Most shelters gladly welcome donations of specific brands of dog, cat, and rabbit food; soft blankets; paper towels; dog treats; and cleaning supplies. As a family, get permission to make and distribute a flyer in your neighborhood, school, or church, asking others to donate specific supplies. On a specified day, gather the supplies and deliver them to the shelter. Pray for families that adopt the shelter animals.

What Does the Bible Say?

"Your righteousness is like the mighty mountains, your justice like the ocean depths. You care for people and animals alike, O LORD. How precious is your unfailing love, O God! All humanity finds shelter in the shadow of your wings" (Psalm 36:6–7 NLT).

Arabic Salad

Stir ingredients together and serve.

1 tomato, minced
1 clove garlic, mashed
2 cucumbers, minced
½ lemon, seeded and chopped fine, rind and all

2 pieces fresh mint, minced
1 small hot pepper, seeded and minced
Salt to taste

Did You Know?

The island of Cyprus, whose name means "copper," has roots to the copper mining industry dating back to biblical times. The Skouriotissa mine covers a large hilly region 35 miles west of the capital of Cyprus. In 12 B.C., it was leased to the highest bidder, King Herod the Great. He was allowed to keep half of the profits mined. The Greek Orthodox Church of Cyprus is currently the owner of this mine, but it is looking to get out of the nonprofitable mining business.

What Can You Do?

The US penny contains copper and zinc. Before 1982, pennies were 95 percent copper and 5 percent zinc. Pennies minted after 1982 are 98 percent zinc and 2 percent copper. When you see pennies on the sidewalk or find them between the sofa cushions, pick them up and put them in a large jar or vase. Ask other family members to contribute their pennies to your collection. When the jar or vase is full, donate your copper (and zinc) to your church.

What Does the Bible Say?

"And He looked up and saw the rich putting their gifts into the treasury. And He saw a poor widow putting in two small copper coins. And He said, "Truly I say to you, this poor widow put in more than all of them" (Luke 21:1–3 NASB).

Israel ....

Matzo Ball Soup

1 (4- to 6-pound) chicken	Water to cover chicken
2 onions, peeled and sliced	2 tablespoons softened butter
3 carrots, scraped and sliced	2 eggs, slightly beaten
3 stalks celery, including leaves, sliced	½ cup matzo meal
3 parsley sprigs	1 teaspoon salt
Salt and pepper to taste	2 tablespoons ice water

Clean chicken. Place in deep pot with onions, carrots, parsley, celery, salt, and pepper. Cover with water. Bring to a boil. Reduce heat and simmer 2½ to 3 hours. Remove chicken and strain soup. With a fork, mix butter and eggs in mixing bowl. Mix in matzo meal and salt. When well blended, add ice water. Cover bowl and refrigerate at least 2 hours. Moisten hands in water and form little matzo balls. Cook balls in clear, strained chicken broth for about 15 minutes or until balls float. Serve with chicken.

Did You Know?

The Medium Is the Matzo was a multimedia art exhibit in New York City created by artist Melissa Shiff in 2005. During this exhibit, square pieces of unleavened matzo bread covered every surface of the art gallery creating a crunchy, multisensory experience for visitors. Jars and jars of matzo balls were stacked to tower above guests. Shiff used this exhibit to share her views about world hunger and the need for action.

What Can You Do?

Every day, 24,000 people die of hunger-related causes worldwide. This number is decreasing each year. People donate food and money to many organizations around the world that make it their business to feed hungry people. Did you know about the Hunger Site (www.thehungersite.com)? When you visit this site, you can click on the Give Free Food button once a day, every day of the year, at no cost to you. Corresponding with the number of people who click the button, sponsors of the site send donations of food staples to countries where hunger prevails. At the site, you can see how many people click the button each day and the amount of food sponsors donate in response.

What Does the Bible Say?

"For I was hungry, and you fed me. I was thirsty, and you gave me a drink. I was a stranger, and you invited me into your home" (Matthew 25:35 NLT).

Mixed Fruit Tzimmes (Fruit Candies)

I pound dried prunes	½ pound dried apples
I pound dried apricots	½ cup honey
I pound dried pineapple	Lemon juice
I pound dried peaches	

Wash fruit. Place in a colander to drain. Put fruit in a large pot, cover with water, and add honey. Cover and cook over low heat. After 20 minutes, test to see if fruit is soft. If it cooks too long, fruit will get mushy. If it tastes too sweet, add a little lemon juice. When fruit cools, add more honey if the fruit is too tart.

Did You Know?

Thousands of years ago, while Moses and the Israelites were hungrily wandering in the desert, God provided manna from heaven. From Bible passages such as Numbers 11:8–9, manna was thought to be a breadlike substance that could be ground, boiled, and made into cakes. However, since we don't have God's recipe for manna, some Jewish scholars believe manna may have been a sticky, honeylike juice that today drops from the sky in May and June from certain shrubs found in the Sinai Desert. Others believe it might have been a secretion from some of the insects that live in shrubbery in the Sinai Desert.

What Can You Do?

OK, so even if you don't have God's recipe for manna, or the right kind of weather to leave honeylike droplets on your doorstep, try making a batch of manna pancakes to serve with your tzimmes. Stir together 2 cups matzo flour, ½ cup boiling water, and 1 tablespoon sesame oil. Knead well on a floured board. Divide into 12 portions and roll out until pancakes are about ¼ inch thick. Cook on a heated, ungreased skillet, turning once to cook both sides. Remove from skillet, and enjoy your manna pancake served with a drizzle of honey.

What Does the Bible Say?

"The manna was like small whitish seeds and tasted like something baked with sweet olive oil. It appeared at night with the dew. In the morning the people would collect the manna, grind or crush it into flour, then boil it and make it into thin wafers" (Numbers 11:7–9 CEV).

Jordan ....

Maqloubeh (Chicken and Vegetables)

2 to 3 cups uncooked rice per chicken
1 head or 2 pounds cauliflower per 1½ chickens, washed and cut into large pieces
Chicken pieces (2 pieces per person)

Salt, pepper, ground cinnamon, allspice
Oil
Hot water (may add bouillon cube) or chicken broth

Sort rice; wash well; soak in salted warm water. Set aside. In a deep pot, boil cauliflower 3 to 4 minutes in salted water; drain. Fry cauliflower in the same pot in 1 inch oil until lightly browned. Drain slightly; place in a bowl. There should be some oil remaining in the pot for the chicken. Spread chicken pieces in tray; sprinkle with ½ teaspoon cinnamon, ½ teaspoon allspice, and ¼ teaspoon black pepper per chicken. Fry chicken lightly in oil on somewhat less heat than was used for frying the cauliflower. Drain slightly; place in another bowl. Pour out the oil. In the deep pot, layer vegetables, chicken pieces, and drained rice. Add hot water or broth until ¼ inch above rice. Cook on medium heat for 5 minutes; reduce heat; simmer until rice is done and water is absorbed. Invert on serving dish. Serve immediately.

Did You Know?

In 2005, the Jordanian Farmers Union (JFU) asked their government to ban the import of live chickens, frozen chickens, and eggs. Jordanian poultry farmers believe their country can meet the demand for chickens and eggs without bringing in foreign chickens! According to the JFU, importing chickens affects poultry farmers and their workers. Jordan produces an estimated 3.3 million chickens and 65 million eggs annually.

What Can You Do?

Play a game of Table Chicken. Take turns staring at each other; see who can stare the longest without blinking. When a champion is determined, talk about items you might not "blink twice about" in your neighborhood: a young child left home alone each day after school; a stray cat needing medical attention; the bushes on the busy street corner that you have to look over and around to see cars in the intersection. As a family, be like the JFU and determine what action you might be able to take regarding one of these issues.

What Does the Bible Say?

"God did this to make all parts of the body work together smoothly, with each part caring about the others. If one part of our body hurts, we hurt all over" (1 Corinthians 12:25–26 CEV).

Mansaf (Chicken and Rice with Yogurt Sauce)

¼ chicken per person
½ to 1 cup uncooked rice per person
Butter/margarine

Jamiid (preserved, sun-dried, and reconstituted yogurt from goat's milk)
Pine nuts and almonds

Salt and spread all chicken pieces with butter and place in a hot oven until the meat turns a pinkish red color (not crispy brown). Set the chicken aside. Measure out the rice and stir it in a skillet with melted butter (about 1 teaspoon per cup) just to coat the rice. Cook rice with 2 cups water for every 1 cup of rice. Wrap pot of rice in a large blanket to keep warm until needed. Heat the jamiid until it begins to boil. Arrange the hot rice on the large serving platter. Top with meat pieces, nuts, and sauce. Everyone eats from the same dish.

Note: *Many children are allergic to nuts. If you are using this book in a group setting, check with parents before serving.*

Did You Know?

Raw goat's milk, only available directly from the goat and usually not from the store down the street, contains digestive enzymes that help people who suffer from Crohn's disease, diabetes, cancer, and autism. But, if you find a goat nearby and don't know its owner, plan on paying big bucks for raw goat's milk. A gallon of raw goat's milk can cost up to $12 in the United States.

What Can You Do?

For $10, less than a gallon of raw goat's milk in the United States, your family can purchase a share of a goat through Heifer International (www.heifer.org). When a family living in poverty receives a goat through Heifer International, they can use that raw goat's milk to drink; make cheese, butter, and yogurt to sell to others; and even use the manure to fertilize a garden. And, because goats have young two to three times a year, Heifer International families are able to start small dairies to help pay for medical expenses, schooling, and additional food. The gift of one small goat has the ability to improve life for an entire family living in another country.

What Does the Bible Say?

"And there will be goats' milk enough for your food, for the food of your household, and sustenance for your maidens" (Proverbs 27:27 NASB)

An American alternate to jamiid:

8 ounces plain yogurt

4 ounces white English cheddar
  cheese (aged), grated

1 teaspoon salt

8 ounces sour cream

1 egg white

2 teaspoons cornstarch

4 cups water

Combine yogurt, sour cream, salt, and cornstarch in a saucepan. Stir with a wooden spoon over low heat. Stir constantly in the same direction. Lightly whisk egg white with fork until frothy and add to yogurt mixture. Continue stirring in the same direction until it boils. Stir approximately 3 minutes until thick. Add cheese, stirring until all cheese melts. Add 4 cups of water and continue stirring in the same direction until boiling.

Moussaka Badinjan (Jordanian Eggplant)

2 pounds eggplant
Salt and pepper to taste
2 small onions, chopped
I pound ground lamb

3 to 4 tomatoes
I tablespoon tomato paste in
I cup water

Cut the eggplant in 1-inch thick slices. Salt and let stand for at least 30 minutes, then wash in cold water and pat dry. Fry until lightly browned. Sauté the chopped onions, and lightly fry the ground lamb. Season to taste. Arrange the eggplant slices and meat in alternate layers with thinly sliced tomatoes. Pour the diluted tomato paste over the layers. Bake in a 350°F oven until nearly all the liquid has evaporated (about 30 minutes). Serve with chopped parsley and/or sautéed pine nuts sprinkled on top.

Did You Know?

This recipe calls for salt and pepper to taste. Have you ever sprinkled a little too much salt on your moussaka? If you know about food that tastes too salty, think about water that tastes salty. Think about the Dead Sea! The Dead Sea, which lies on the Jordanian border, has four times the salt content of any of the world's oceans. Being 1,300 feet below sea level, its water contains more industrial salt, table salt, and minerals than any other body of water in the world. That means that the water is so thick, you can read a newspaper while lying on your back in the middle of the Dead Sea and not have to worry about using a water float!

What Can You Do?

The next time a family member loses a tooth, has oral surgery, or has sores in his or her mouth, mix 1 tablespoon of salt into eight ounces of warm water. Have him rinse his mouth thoroughly, making sure not to swallow the Dead Sea–like water. The person will not have to wait long for healing to begin. Talk about Mark 9:50 and what it means to have "salt in yourselves, and be at peace with each other." Pray together as a family for healing of mouths, souls, hearts, and minds.

What Does the Bible Say?

"Salt is good, but if it loses its saltiness, how can you make it salty again? Have salt in yourselves, and be at peace with each other" (Mark 9:50 NIV).

Stuffed Pita Pockets

2 tablespoons butter or margarine
1 medium onion, chopped
1 pound ground beef
1 teaspoon salt
½ teaspoon pepper

2 tablespoons parsley, chopped
2 medium tomatoes, chopped
1 pita loaf for each sandwich
Lettuce

Melt butter or margarine in frying pan. Sauté the onion for 5 minutes. Add meat, salt, pepper, parsley, and tomatoes. Mix well. Cook over medium heat. Stir until meat browns. Cut each pita loaf in half and stuff pocket with lettuce and meat mixture.

Did You Know?

Jordan is a country known for its hospitality. It is very common for desert-dwelling Jordanian families to welcome complete strangers into their homes. These families realize that by showing hospitality to others, they may someday receive needed services from others. Food, water, and shelter in the harsh desert climate are always welcome.

What Can You Do?

As a family, read Genesis 18:1–8. Talk about the many ways in which Abraham showed hospitality to the three visitors. Do you think Abraham realized who the strangers were? Talk about ways your family shows hospitality to others. How can your family show hospitality to strangers today? What are some ways you might be hospitable to strangers without inviting them into your home? Why might our hospitality to strangers be different from the hospitality the Jordanian people show to strangers? What may hold us back? Close your discussion by reading Hebrews 13:2.

What Does the Bible Say?

"Don't forget to welcome strangers. By doing that, some people have welcomed angels without knowing it" (Hebrews 13:2 NIrV).

Lebanon ·· ·· ·· ··

Hummus (Chickpea Dip)

I (15-ounce) can garbanzo beans (chickpeas)
¼ cup sesame seed paste (also known as tahini)
3 tablespoons lemon juice
¼ teaspoon ground cumin
I clove garlic, chopped
Salt and pepper to taste
Pita bread, torn into pieces

Drain garbanzo beans and save the liquid. Place beans in a food processor or blender. Blend beans until smooth. Add sesame seed paste, lemon juice, ground cumin, and garlic. Blend again until smooth, adding reserved liquid as needed. Season with salt and pepper to taste. Mixture should be the consistency of a dip. To eat, scoop it up with pita bread.

Did You Know?

Traditional music of Lebanon is a unique combination of melodies and intricate rhythms. These unique melodies come from equally unique instruments. The *oud* is a 12-stringed instrument played with an eagle's feather. The *tablah* is goat or fish skin stretched over a vase-shaped drum and played between the legs. The *nay* is an open-ended pipe with six holes for the fingers and one hole for the thumb. The force used to blow through the *nay* determines the octave played. The *ganun* is a flat, trapezoid instrument with up to 81 strings, similar to a dulcimer. Because the *ganun* is so difficult to play, many Lebanese orchestras have replaced it with the piano. When your mom tells you to go practice the piano, remember that there are harder instruments to learn to play!

What Can You Do?

Plan your own family worship service. If someone in your family plays an instrument, have him or her select a song for you to sing. You'll need one person to deliver a short sermon (children love to volunteer for this!); someone to read a selected Bible passage; another person to offer a prayer; and, of course, you will need an usher to direct family members to chairs and take the offering.

What Does the Bible Say?

"Praise God in his sanctuary; praise him in his mighty heavens.
Praise him for his acts of power; praise him for his surpassing greatness.
Praise him with the sounding of the trumpet, praise him with the harp and lyre.
Praise him with tambourine and dancing, praise him with the strings and flute.
Praise him with the clash of cymbals, praise him with resounding cymbals.
Let everything that has breath praise the Lord. Praise the Lord" (Psalm 150 NIV).

United Arab Emirates......

Mujadarra (Lentils and Rice)

3 medium yellow onions, diced   I cup uncooked rice
2 tablespoons oil   2 teaspoons salt
I cup lentils

In large skillet, sauté diced onions in hot oil. When browned, set aside. In a large covered pot, place lentils and 3½ cups cold water. Bring to boil, turn down to simmer, and cook 15 minutes. Add cooked onion, rice, and salt. Cover and simmer 20 minutes until rice and lentils are soft. If a bit of water remains unabsorbed, remove from heat, and let stand 5 minutes or until it soaks in. To serve, place pita bread on a cookie sheet and bake in a 350°F oven until crisp. Crumble pita bread into individual serving bowls. Top with lentil and rice mixture. Serve with plain yogurt.

Did You Know?

Seven sheikhdoms, land owned by one ruling family, comprise the United Arab Emirates. Each February, the sheikhdom of Dubai holds the Dubai Shopping Festival. This festival lasts for one month and includes activities for the entire family. Cultural displays of traditional crafts, clothing, music, and dance are popular. The Carpet Oasis is a favorite spot during the festival. Here shoppers can find thousands of handmade oriental and Persian rugs all under one roof. And, just in case you want to shop for some popular name-brand products, the Dubai Shopping Festival is said to have "the world's best brands at the world's lowest prices!"

What Can You Do?

After dinner, discuss ways your family can anonymously share gifts of food, toys, books, or clothing to someone you know who is in need. Then pack up the family and head out for a shopping spree for that special someone. Make a rule that during the shopping spree no one will purchase anything for a member of your family. Stay focused on the person in need. When you go to deliver the gifts, park your car around the corner from the person's house and quietly set the gift on their front steps. Ring the doorbell and quickly run away. Watch the front door from a secret place. Don't forget to attach a gift tag that includes one of your family's favorite Bible verses.

What Does the Bible Say?

"Why is everyone hungry for more? 'More, more,' they say. 'More, more.' I have God's more-than-enough, more joy in one ordinary day than they get in all their shopping sprees. At day's end I'm ready for sound sleep, for you, God, have put my life back together" (Psalm 4:6–8 The Message).

Stirring Up a World of Fun in

a World of Fun in

NORTH AMERICA

Canada
United States

Canada . . . .

Canadian Blueberry Dessert

4 cups blueberries
2 tablespoons lemon juice
½ cup packed brown sugar
2 teaspoons cornstarch
⅔ cup quick-cooking oats

½ cup plain flour
⅓ cup packed brown sugar
Dash of salt
⅓ cup margarine or butter
Vanilla ice cream

Toss blueberries with lemon juice in ungreased 1½-quart casserole dish. Mix ½ cup brown sugar and the cornstarch; stir into blueberries. Mix separately oats, flour, ⅓ cup brown sugar and the salt; cut in margarine with fork. Sprinkle over blueberry mixture. Bake uncovered at 350°F oven until topping is light brown and blueberries are bubbly, about 40 minutes. Serve warm with ice cream.

Did You Know?

In Nova Scotia, Canada, blueberries have grown wild for hundreds of years. Blueberries used to be called star berries because of the star-shaped tip on each berry. Blueberries are harvested using handheld rakes or with machine harvesters. Once picked, the berries are placed into a winder, which removes leaves and sticks. The scalper then washes out the stones and dirt before the berries are shuttled through a freezing tunnel and quick frozen in only 11 minutes. After the berries are frozen, the destemmer removes any stems that are still attached to the berries.

What Can You Do?

For a fun family art project, boil together 1 cup blueberries with 2 cups milk. Boil until the milk becomes a beautiful blue-gray colored paint. Let the paint cool a few minutes before pouring through a strainer. Using a foam brush, spread an even coat of paint on white cardstock to create a cloudy, gray sky. Embellish the picture with scenery stickers, cotton balls, and construction paper cutouts to illustrate a shepherd searching for his lost sheep on a cloudy day. And just in case you wondered, early American colonialists made paint this very same way to paint their houses.

What Does the Bible Say?

"I will be like a shepherd looking for his scattered flock. I will find my sheep and rescue them from all the places to which they were scattered on that dark and cloudy day" (Ezekiel 34:12 NLT).

Canadian Butter Tarts

1 cup plain flour
¾ cup margarine or butter,
   softened and divided (½ cup
   and ¼ cup)
¼ cup powdered sugar
¾ cup packed brown sugar

¼ cup dark corn syrup
1 egg, slightly beaten
¼ teaspoon salt
¼ cup currants or chopped
   raisins

Heat oven to 350°F. Mix flour, ½ cup margarine, and the powdered sugar. Divide into 24 equal pieces, and create a lining for small ungreased muffin cups by pressing each piece against the bottom and side of the muffin cup. Do not allow pastry to come above tops of cups. Mix brown sugar and ¼ cup margarine. Stir in corn syrup, egg, salt, and currants. Spoon mixture into each muffin cup. Bake until filling is set and crust is light brown, about 20 minutes. Cool in muffin cups 20 minutes. Remove from muffin cups with tip of knife. Cool on a wire rack.

Did You Know?

Samuel de Champlain was the first recorded Canadian dairy farmer in 1610. Today, there are approximately 1.3 million milk-producing cows in Canada. The average dairy farm has 47 cows, with each cow weighing about 1,300 pounds. After a cow has given birth to her first calf, around the age of two, she is milked for ten months. Then she is given a rest for several months before her next calf is born. Dairy cows look thin because most of the food they eat becomes milk, instead of muscle or fat.

What Can You Do?

OK, as you are sipping a glass of milk and enjoying your Canadian butter tarts after dinner, work together as a family to do this milk math. If there are 1.3 million milk-producing cows in Canada, and the average cow produces 200 gallons of milk in a month, how many gallons of milk can a cow produce in a day? How many 8-ounce glasses of milk would one cow produce in a day? How many 8-ounce glasses of milk does your family drink in a day? How many total gallons of milk are produced in Canada in a year? Whew! And, when you are finished, thank God for milk and for the cows that produce it in an amazing way!

What Does the Bible Say?

"We went into the land you sent us to. It really does have plenty of milk and honey!" (Numbers 13:27 NIrV).

Canadian Flapjacks

2 cups flour	**2 eggs**
1 pinch sea salt	**½ cup honey**
1½ cups apple juice or milk	**2 teaspoons baking power**
2 tablespoons oil	**1 Pippin apple, grated**

Combine all ingredients except apple with mixer. Add apple and mix by hand. Spoon into oiled frying pan over medium heat. Turn when bubbles appear and harden. Brown other side. Serve immediately with your favorite syrup or topping.

Did You Know?

Canada's newest territory, Nunavut, meaning "our land," officially split from the Canadian Northwest Territories on April 1, 1999. Although this new territory covers almost 730,000 square miles of mostly arctic tundra, only 29,000 people, mostly native Inuit, live there. This land has only one paved road and 27 times more caribou than people. Vegetation is about as sparse as the population, with only moss, small willow shrubs, and tough grass being able to grow in a small portion of the territory. Nunavut will probably not be your next destination for a family camping trip!

What Can You Do?

On a clear night, gather the family together and sit in the backyard or go to a park or field away from city lights. Listen to the night noises and the silence of the evening. Take along a book of star constellations; a flashlight; and, most definitely, some insect repellent. Search out the constellations and enjoy the beauty of the night. Enjoy the stillness, the calm, and the quiet. When was the last time you really listened to "quiet"? Before going inside, take a few minutes to pray together for the people in the world who do not know God, the Creator of the universe.

What Does the Bible Say?

"Be still, and know that I am God; I will be exalted among the nations, I will be exalted in the earth" (Psalm 46:10 AMP).

Tourtiere (Canadian Pork Pie)

1 pound ground pork	¼ teaspoon ground sage
1 medium onion, chopped	¼ teaspoon pepper
1 clove garlic, chopped	⅛ teaspoon ground cloves
½ cup water	1 egg
1½ teaspoons salt	Pastry for double-crust pie, pur-
½ teaspoon dried thyme leaves	chased

Combine all ingredients except pastry in a large, heavy saucepan. Heat to boiling, stirring constantly. Reduce heat, and continue cooking and stirring until meat is browned but still moist. Heat oven to 425°F. Prepare bottom pastry according to manufacturer's instructions. Pour meat mixture over the bottom pastry. Cover with top pastry. Seal edge by pressing around edge with a fork. Cut slits in top to let steam escape. Bake until top is brown, 30 to 40 minutes. If edge becomes too brown, cover with a strip of foil. Let pie stand 10 minutes before cutting.

Did You Know?

In 2000, Toronto city officials issued a Moose Call to boost the sagging tourism industry and to draw attention to Toronto in their bid for the 2008 Olympics. Local Toronto artists decorated 326 large fiberglass moose and placed the herd around the city. The plan was to auction off the moose statues at the end of moose season, with some of the proceeds going to the Canadian Olympic team. However, many of the statues were vandalized, and city critics determined that plaid moose weren't really much of a tourist draw.

What Can You Do?

Have you ever thought you had a really great idea only to be discouraged by others who thought it was ridiculous? As a family, discuss ways you can speak a little more kindly and behave a little more compassionately. Start a list of completely tactful and caring responses. Post the list on the refrigerator and practice communicating kindly and with love. Then, the next time a member of your family thinks that it would be a great idea to paint your house bright pink, or that the best television programs are on after midnight, refer to the list and consider your response.

What Does the Bible Say?

"Kind words are like honey—sweet to the soul and healthy for the body" (Proverbs 16:24 NLT).

Apple Pie

¼ **cup sugar**
1 **tablespoon plain flour**
½ **teaspoon cinnamon**
Dash of salt
4 **cups peeled and sliced apples**

¼ **cup butter**
¾ **cup brown sugar**
½ **cup unsifted plain flour**
Pastry for double-crust pie, purchased

Line pie plate with bottom pastry. Blend sugar, flour, cinnamon, and salt. Toss lightly with apples. Spoon into unbaked bottom pastry. Combine butter, brown sugar, and flour. Sprinkle over pie filling. Cover with pastry top. Cut slits in top. Bake in 425°F oven 35 to 40 minutes or until top is brown.

Did You Know?

More than 7,000 varieties of apples are grown within the United States. Besides being a tasty treat, apples have been used throughout the ages to predict love and to celebrate marriage. In ancient times, couples would dodge apples instead of rice as they left the church. (Ouch!) In Ireland, apple bobbing was helpful if a person was trying to determine whom to marry. And if apple bobbing didn't help, a person could throw apple peels over her shoulder to form the first initial of her future spouse's name. A couple sharing an apple in seventh-century Greece was a symbol of engagement and marriage in the year to come.

What Can You Do?

If your family is not in the habit of daily devotions, start small. Begin the day by reading just one Bible verse, one morsel of God's Word. (*Stirring Up a World of Fun* has 100 verses to get you started!) Meditate on that verse through out the day. Think of ways you see that Bible verse working in your life throughout the day. Commit the verse to memory. Before going to bed each night, write the verse in a spiral notebook.

What Does the Bible Say?

"But the fruit the Holy Spirit produces is love, joy and peace. It is being patient, kind and good. It is being faithful and gentle and having control of oneself" (Galatians 5:22–23 NIrV).

Bacalaitos (Fish Snack)

½ pound codfish
2 cups flour
½ teaspoon baking powder
½ teaspoon salt

½ teaspoon garlic powder
White pepper to taste
1½ cups cold water
Oil

Cut codfish into small pieces. Combine flour, baking powder, and salt. Add codfish, garlic powder, and white pepper. Mix well. Add water. Set aside 10 to 15 minutes. Drop the mixture by tablespoonfuls into hot oil. Turn once or twice. Fry until golden brown.

Did You Know?

About a one-hour boat ride from Puerto Rico's main island is the quarter-mile-wide Phosphorescent Bay, known for the best night swimming ever. The bay is filled with dinoflagellates, microscopic one-celled organisms, a form of algae. When in the water, the slightest movement causes these microorganisms to light up in an aqua green glow. So, if you decide to visit, and decide to go for a little night swim, try lying on your back to create a glowing snow angel. Or raise your hand above the water and watch tiny bits of light fall back into the bay. At last count, Puerto Rico's Phosphorescent Bay has 700,000 dinoflagellates per gallon of water!

What Can You Do?

Serve green or blue fruit-flavored drink mix with dinner tonight to remind family members of the microscopic algae in Puerto Rico's Phosphorescent Bay. Discuss microorganisms and other minute details in the world that only God could create. When was the last time you thought about the individual water droplets that help form a rainbow? Can you imagine the world without the weightless particles that create light? Give thanks to God for His amazing creation—the biggest and the smallest portions of it.

What Does the Bible Say?

"When I see the rainbow in the clouds, I will remember the eternal covenant between God and every living creature on earth" (Genesis 9:16 NLT).

Brownies

**2 (1-ounce) squares unsweet-
ened chocolate
½ cup butter or margarine
1 cup sugar
2 eggs**

**1 teaspoon vanilla
½ cup sifted flour
½ cup pecans, chopped
(optional)**

Melt chocolate in top of a double boiler. Cream butter and sugar. Add eggs and beat well. Blend in melted chocolate, vanilla, and sifted flour. Add nuts if you wish. Pour batter into a greased 8-by-8-by-2-inch pan. Bake at 325°F for 35 minutes.

Did You Know?

January 22 is National Blonde Brownie Day. But, if you are partial to ooey, gooey chocolate brownies (with nuts, of course), you should visit Okmulgee, Oklahoma, during June. Okmulgee is the world's record holder for the biggest pecan brownie, the biggest pecan pie, the biggest pecan cookie, and the biggest ice cream and cookie party. Okmulgee, the home of the Oklahoma Pecan Festival, is known as a "great place to discover the nuttier times."

What Can You Do?

As a family, talk about "the biggest and bests" in your life. Does your family own the biggest house on the block? Does the teenager in your home think she has to have the best brand of jeans before school begins each fall? Read Luke 22:7–29 from the Bible. What "biggest and best" were the disciples disagreeing about in this passage? How should we respond to wanting "the biggest and the best" of worldly things? How did Jesus respond in the Luke passage? What "best" did Jesus provide for us? How would our lives look different if we wanted the "biggest and best" of Jesus?

What Does the Bible Say?

"Foreign kings order their people around, and powerful rulers call themselves everyone's friends. But don't be like them. The most important one of you should be like the least important, and your leader should be like a servant" (Luke 22:25–26 CEV).

Chili

½ cup onion, chopped
1 pound ground beef
1 can tomato soup
1 teaspoon salt

4 teaspoons chili powder
¼ teaspoon black pepper
1 (16-ounce) can red kidney
beans

Place chopped onion and ground beef in heavy skillet. Cook until meat browns. Stir frequently so there will be no lumps of meat. Add other ingredients. Simmer 20 to 30 minutes. Top with grated cheese, if desired.

Did You Know?

There are many stories about the origin of chili. All of them lead back to Texas, definitely not Mexico. A translation from the *Diccionario de Mejicanismos (Mexican Dictionary)*, published in 1959, describes chili as: "A detestable food passing itself off as Mexican, sold in the US from Texas to New York." One of the earliest origins of chili goes back to the Texas cattle drives in the 1800s when a hearty meal needed to be made from food available along the trail and the dried beef carried by the cowboys.

What Can You Do?

Place the spices in the recipe above in a snack-sized resealable bag, substituting 2 tablespoons of dehydrated onions for the fresh onion. Seal the plastic bag and shake to combine. Decorate a lunch-sized paper bag with Bible passages, witty sayings, and colorful drawings. Write on the bag: *Add 1 pound of cooked ground beef to this chili-in-a-bag.* Place in the paper bag one can of tomato soup, one can of kidney beans, and the plastic bag of spices. As a family, deliver your chili-in-a-bag to a neighbor, a nearby fire station, or a family in your church who may need the makings of a meal. Pray for the people who received your chili-in-a-bag when you come home.

What Does the Bible Say?

"If you have two coats, give one to the poor. If you have food, share it with those who are hungry" (Luke 3:11 *NLT*).

Chocolate Chip Cookies

1 cup butter
¾ cup sugar
¾ cup brown sugar, packed
1 teaspoon vanilla
½ teaspoon water
2 eggs

2¼ cups sifted flour
1 teaspoon baking soda
1 teaspoon salt
1 (12-ounce) package semisweet chocolate chips

Blend butter, sugars, vanilla, and water. Beat in eggs. Add dry ingredients. Stir in chips. Drop by half teaspoonfuls on greased cookie sheet. Bake at 375°F for 10 to 12 minutes.

Did You Know?

In the 1930s, Ruth Wakefield, who was the co-owner of the Toll House Inn, was making her famous butter drop dough cookies when she discovered she only had a Nestlé semisweet chocolate bar, not the regular baker's chocolate called for in the recipe. She cut the chocolate bar into bits and added them to her regular butter cookie recipe, inventing the chocolate chip cookie. Andrew Nestlé and Ruth Wakefield struck a deal as sales of chocolate bars grew because of Wakefield's recipe. Nestlé agreed to always print the Toll House recipe on its packaging and Ruth Wakefield agreed to a lifetime supply of Nestlé chocolate.

What Can You Do?

Invent your own family board game. Brainstorm ideas from each member. Incorporate something from everyone into one game. The game board could be created on the inside of a flattened cereal box, on a brown paper bag, or if you are really thinking outside the box, how about on all four sides of a milk carton, or drawn on a large piece of freezer paper taped to the wall? Create fun place markers that coordinate with the theme of the game. Use a spinner from one of your other games or create a draw deck from index cards that contain instructions for each player's move across the board. When the game is complete, enjoy playing it together.

What Does the Bible Say?

"His brother's name was Jubal, the first musician—the inventor of the harp and flute" (Genesis 4:21 NLT).

Date Banana Pudding Parfaits

1 package (3.4-ounce) vanilla pudding mix
2 cups 1 percent lowfat milk
1¼ cups plain lowfat yogurt
¾ cup California dates
1 banana, mashed

1 cup crushed chocolate wafer cookies
California dates, pitted, for garnish
Fresh mint sprigs, for garnish

Using a whisk, blend pudding mix, milk, and yogurt. Stir in dates and banana. Layer ¼ cup pudding in the bottom of each of 4, 8-ounce dessert glasses. Sprinkle 2 tablespoons cookie crumbs on top of each. Layer in another ¼ cup pudding and another 2 tablespoons cookie crumbs. Top each with remaining pudding. Garnish with additional dates and mint sprig just before serving, if desired.

Did You Know?

Dates have been around a long time! Date stones found in Egypt have dated back to 4500 B.C. However, date palms have only been in the United States since the last century. The average date palm tree produces around 100 pounds of dates a year, with some trees producing 300 to 600 pounds each year. Date palms can live up to 100 years! Just think, over its 100-year life span, one date palm can produce 60,000 pounds of fruit. To put things into perspective, a large dump truck, or a full-grown humpback whale, weighs only about 30,000 pounds!

What Can You Do?

As a family, plant a small tree in your yard. As your family grows, watch the tree grow too! Check out the really cool National Arbor Day Foundation Web site (www.arbor-day.org), and look for tree-care information, pruning, and planting tips. If your family cannot plant a tree, consider making a donation to the National Arbor Day Foundation. Each $5 donation funds the planting of a tree in a national forest, helping to restore forests damaged by fire, insects, or disease.

What Does the Bible Say?

"But blessed is the man who trusts in the Lord, whose confidence is in him. He will be like a tree planted by the water that sends out its roots by the stream. It does not fear when heat comes; its leaves are always green. It has no worries in a year of drought and never fails to bear fruit" (Jeremiah 17:7–8 NIV).

Fried Chicken

1 cup flour	**½ teaspoon pepper**
1 teaspoon salt	**1 chicken fryer, cut up**
½ teaspoon paprika	

Mix flour, salt, paprika, and pepper. Dip pieces of chicken in flour mixture. Fry in hot oil until golden brown and tender (about 10 to 12 minutes on each side).

Did You Know?

In 1930, Colonel Harland Sanders of Kentucky Fried Chicken fame created southern fried chicken fast-food style by using the then new invention, the pressure cooker. He found the pressure cooker to be a more efficient way of cooking chicken, rather than a skillet, which made people wait for at least 30 minutes before eating. For years, Colonel Sanders carried the secret recipe for his chicken in his head and the spice mixture in his car. Today, only a few people know the recipe—and they're not talking.

What Can You Do?

Play a family fun game of Tell Me a Secret. Whisper the Bible verse below in the ear of another family member. They in turn whisper what they heard into another family member's ear. Continue in the same manner until the last person repeats aloud what he has heard. The Bible verse may end up no longer the New International Reader's Version, but rather someone's own translation. Repeat the game with other simple verses, reinforcing the correct verse at the end of each round.

What Does the Bible Say?

"Those who talk about others tell secrets. But those who can be trusted keep things to themselves" (Proverbs 11:13 NIrV).

Grilled Cheese Sandwiches

8 slices bread   **Butter**
4 slices American cheese

Butter one side of each slice of bread. Place one slice of American cheese between slices. Be sure buttered side is out. Brown slightly on both sides in frying pan over low heat.

Did You Know?

The next time you decide to make a grilled cheese sandwich, look at it closely before taking that first bite. Ten years ago, Diana Duyser sat down to eat her lunch of a home-made grilled cheese sandwich. After taking the first bite, she noticed that the grill marks on the bread looked remarkably like the face of the Virgin Mary. So, she put the slightly nibbled sandwich in a clear plastic box, surrounded it by cotton balls, and kept it on her nightstand. Today, ten years later, the sandwich is free of mold, and the face of Mary still visible. Diana is convinced the sandwich has brought her fame, fortune, and good luck for the last ten years.

What Can You Do?

As a family, talk about some of the common items that people use or activities they engage in that they believe will bring them good luck. Do you know someone who feels lucky because he or she carries a special rock in his or her pocket or because he or she avoided walking under a ladder or breaking a mirror? Discuss the difference between relying on luck and in trusting God. Read the Bible story of King Saul and the Witch of Endor found in 1 Samuel 28:3–20. Why had King Saul fallen out of favor with God? Why was David "a man after God's own heart"? Read David's Psalm 32 for a clue as to the heart of David.

What Does the Bible Say?

"So I confessed my sins and told them all to you. I said, 'I'll tell the Lord each one of my sins.' Then you forgave me and took away my guilt" (Psalm 32:5 CEV).

Louisiana Cream Fudge

3 cups granulated sugar   **¼ cup butter**
2 cups whipping cream   **½ cup flour**
1 cup cornstarch   **2 cups whole pecan halves**

Put the sugar, whipping cream, and cornstarch in a saucepan. Using a candy thermometer, cook to the soft ball stage. Remove the pan from the heat. Add the butter. Beat with a mixer for 5 minutes. Blend in the flour. Continue beating until the candy is creamy and thick. Add the pecans. Beat until thick. Pour into a buttered 13-by-9-inch pan or platter. When it is cool, cut it into pieces.

Did You Know?

Your teeth can be considered weapons! According to Louisiana law, a person who bites someone with his or her teeth commits assault. However, biting someone with false teeth becomes a more serious crime—aggravated assault. Keep your teeth where they belong, and brush your "weapons" after eating a piece of Louisiana cream fudge!

What Can You Do?

When was the last time your family sat down to discuss some of the expectations, rules, or laws you have in your home? Are there some rules that need repeating or put in writing so that they are easier for everyone to remember? Do you need some new rules because the children in the family are getting older? After the family discussion, end with a group hug and a verbal affirmation for each family member.

What Does the Bible Say?

"The Law of the LORD is perfect; it gives us new life. His teachings last forever, and they give wisdom to ordinary people" (Psalm 19:7 CEV).

Macaroni and Cheese

1 (8-ounce) package macaroni
6 cups water
1 teaspoon salt
¼ cup butter or margarine

¼ cup milk
¼ pound Cheddar cheese, grated
Salt and pepper to taste

Add macaroni to 6 cups boiling water with 1 teaspoon salt. Stir. Boil rapidly, stirring occasionally, for 7 to 10 minutes. Drain. Add butter, milk, and cheese. Mix well. Add salt and pepper to taste. Pour into small casserole dish. Bake at 350°F for 30 minutes, or until hot and bubbly.

Did You Know?

Some historians believe that Thomas Jefferson, the third President of the United States, created macaroni and cheese. Historians also report that Thomas Jefferson served the dish to guests in the White House in 1802. However, macaroni and cheese really became popular in 1937, when Kraft Foods introduced Americans to the buy-it-in-a-box style of macaroni and cheese. Today, Kraft reports that it sells more than 1 million boxes of macaroni and cheese every day.

What Can You Do?

Macaroni comes in so many unique shapes and sizes. For a family craft activity, cut a 3-inch circle of stiff white cardstock for each member. If you don't have cardstock, cut circles from an empty cereal box. Punch a hole on the upper edge of each of the circles. Use macaroni shapes to create and glue snowflake designs on the cardstock. When the glue is dry, spray paint the snowflakes with white spray paint. Thread a piece of yarn through the hole and hang these unique, one-of-a-kind snowflakes around your house or on a Christmas tree.

What Does the Bible Say?

"God's voice is glorious in the thunder. We cannot comprehend the greatness of his power. He directs the snow to fall on the earth and tells the rain to pour down" (Job 37:5–6 NLT).

Magic Peanut Butter Pie

1 (8-inch) baked pie crust	1 box instant vanilla pudding
1 cup powdered sugar	1 (8-ounce) container whipped
½ cup peanut butter	topping

Mix powdered sugar and ½ cup peanut butter until crumbly. Pour ¾ of the crumbs on pie crust, bottom and sides. Mix pudding as directed and pour on pie crust. Let set up. Spread whipped topping on top and sprinkle with the rest of the crumbs. Cool for several hours before serving.

Did You Know?

One-half of the peanuts grown in the United States are used to make peanut butter and peanut spreads. George Washington Carver was a great scientist and researcher. He discovered 300 uses for peanuts and hundreds of uses for soybeans, pecans, and sweet potatoes. He gave his discoveries to mankind without asking for anything in return. When people asked him why didn't patent or profit from his products, he said, "God gave them to me. How can I sell them to someone else?"

What Can You Do?

Gather enough pinecones for each member of your family to have at least one. After dinner, let family members roll their pine cones in peanut butter then in bird seeds, making bird feeders. Attach a wire to the top of each pinecone bird feeder for a hanger. Take your bird feeders outside, hang them in the trees, and watch the birds eat from your pinecones all week.

What Does the Bible Say?

"The earth is the Lord's, and everything in it, the world, and all who live in it" (Psalm 24:1 NIV).

Orange Frost

½ cup orange juice
½ banana, frozen
1 tablespoon nonfat milk
   powder

Dash of cinnamon or nutmeg
2 ice cubes

Place all ingredients into a blender. Blend until creamy. Divide mixture between 2 chilled glasses.

Did You Know?

Even though oranges originally came from Southeast Asia, the United States is now the major producer of oranges in the world. Which came first, the fruit or the color? The word *orange* comes from the Indian language of Sanskrit, and means "fragrant." The Chinese believe that orange peels aid in digestion. In medieval times, people believed that the scent of oranges had a calming effect.

What Can You Do?

Place an unpeeled orange on the table when you sit down to dinner. After dinner, take turns peeling the orange and splitting it into sections. Distribute the sections evenly to all family members. Have each member pray the same number of prayer items as orange sections he or she received. Focus prayer items on wrong actions of the day and the need for forgiveness from all involved. When the prayer is finished, enjoy the sweet taste of God's loving forgiveness as you savor each orange section.

What Does the Bible Say?

"How far has the Lord taken our sins from us? Farther than the distance from east to west" (Psalm 103:12 CEV).

Strawberry Freezers

14 fresh strawberries
½ cup frozen limeade concen-
trate

½ cup water
6 ice cubes

Rinse the strawberries and cut off the tops. Put all of the ingredients into a blender and blend on high until smooth. Pour into glasses and enjoy!

Did You Know?

Botanists do not consider the strawberry to be a true berry. True berries have seeds on the inside, not on the outside like the strawberry. Besides being tasty and healthy, strawberry juice can cool people who have a fever. Strawberry juice combined with honey and rubbed onto the skin can help when you have had a little too much sun. But, don't just lick off the sticky concoction; for the best effect, you should rinse off with warm water and a little lemon juice. How about slathering on some leftover strawberry freezer?

What Can You Do?

An average strawberry has approximately 200 seeds. Begin a 200 List of people you and your family know who need prayer. Be sure to include friends or family members who are ill, lonely, or need direction in their lives. You might want to add people to the list who are celebrating the birth of a new child, a new marriage, or a new job. Be sure to include each member of your immediate family too. By the end of the week, do you have 200 people to pray for?

What Does the Bible Say?

"Always be joyful. Pray continually, and give thanks whatever happens. This is what God wants for you in Christ Jesus" (1 Thessalonians 5:16–18 NCV).

Stirring Up a World of Fun in

SOUTH AMERICA

Argentina	Costa Rica	Honduras	Venezuela
Chile	Guatemala	Paraguay	
Columbia	Haiti	Peru	

Argentina ....

Dulce de Leche (Milk Jam)

Place an unopened can of sweetened condensed milk in a medium saucepan (remove the label first). Cover the can with water plus 1 to 2 more inches. Simmer for 4 hours, making sure the can is always completely covered with water. (If not, the can could explode!) Let the can cool, and then open and serve. Use as an icing for cakes, cookies, or graham crackers, or as a topping for ice cream.

Did You Know?

Argentina is a land of cattle! In 1880, Holando-Argentino cattle began to be imported to Argentina from Holland. This breed was used for beef, as well as for milk production. Holando-Argentino cattle can travel over three miles a day, eating native grasses and producing about eight gallons of milk every day during a female cow's milking period. And, if you are a big beef eater, Argentina is the place to go! A meal in Argentina consists of mostly beef, with maybe a few vegetables for color!

What Can You Do?

Play a fun game of Solid Food Search. Form two teams. Each team will need a Bible, a glass of milk for each member of the team, and a list of the following Bible verses. Teams will race to find a Bible verse, read it aloud to each other, and then take one swallow from their glasses of milk. The first team to finish its milk is the winner. The team that still has milk left in its glasses, can pour dulce de leche in their milk and savor the flavor while reading God's Word!

1 Corinthians 1:4	Romans 12:9
Psalm 119:2	Psalm 51:10
Luke 6:21	Colossians 3:1–2
1 Peter 2:2	

What Does the Bible Say?

"A person who is living on milk isn't very far along in the Christian life and doesn't know much about doing what is right. Solid food is for those who are mature, who have trained themselves to recognize the difference between right and wrong and then do what is right" (Hebrews 5:13–14 NLT).

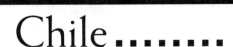

Chile ....

Pastel de Choclo (Corn Pie)

3 eggs, boiled and chopped into medium-sized pieces
20 black olives

¾ teaspoon black pepper
½ cup raisins
¼ teaspoon cumin

Pino:
¼ cup oil
4 cups onion, chopped
2 large cloves garlic, finely chopped
2 pounds ground beef
2 teaspoons salt

Corn:
3 packages frozen corn
½ teaspoon salt
2 tablespoons sugar
1½ teaspoons sweet basil
2 cups milk
¼ pound butter

Pour oil in a skillet; cook onions over high heat until transparent. Mix beef and salt with onions. Cook until you don't see the pink in the meat anymore. Add pepper, raisins, and cumin; cook for 5 minutes. Place 3 packages of frozen corn in bowl. Add salt, sugar, and basil; mix well. Drop corn 1 cup at a time through the hole in the top of a blender. Add milk ¼ cup at a time to help the corn grind completely. In a pot on the stove, melt ¼ pound butter and add the ground corn mixture; cook, stirring constantly for 30 minutes, until thick. Spread pino in 12 small baking dishes. Add in order: olives, boiled eggs, and corn mixture. On top, sprinkle 1 tablespoon sugar and ¼ cup butter cut in pieces. Bake at 400°F for 45 minutes or until browned on top.

Did You Know?

Punta Arenas, Chile, on the southernmost tip of Chile, lies directly under the paper-thin Antarctic ozone hole, which is more than 28.5 million square kilometers in size (three times larger than the US mainland). It poses serious health risks to the residents of Punta Arenas and other southern Chilean cities because of increased exposure to the sun's ultraviolet rays.

What Can You Do?

Global warming, long-range climate change, affects all of us. Greenhouse gases that harm the atmospheric ozone result from people living in the world. Help decrease these effects: turn off lights when you leave a room; recycle cans, plastic, and paper to cut down on manufacturing; plant more trees that release good gases into the air. Discuss more ways your family can help protect the atmosphere for future generations.

What Does the Bible Say?

"God spoke: 'Let us make human beings in our image, make them reflecting our nature. So they can be responsible for the fish in the sea, the birds in the air, the cattle, and, yes, Earth itself, and every animal that moves on the face of Earth'" (Genesis 1:26 The Message).

Sopaipillas

| 1 cup flour | 3 tablespoons shortening |
| 1 teaspoon salt | ½ cup of lukewarm water |

Mix flour, salt, and shortening with water. Knead and then let rest for 15 minutes. Roll dough very thin and cut into 3-inch circles with a cookie cutter. Fry in 3 inches of hot oil until puffy and golden brown. Serve hot with honey.

Did You Know?

Authentic Chilean sopaipillas are made and served in two different ways depending on the region of Chile. Sopaipillas from northern Chile are fried pastries cut in circles. The dough usually contains pureed pumpkin, and they are served with sweet, sticky molasses. Traditionally, this authentic northern Chilean dessert is made on a rainy day as a special treat. Sopaipillas in southern Chile are made like the recipe above. Instead of a dessert, sopaipillas from southern Chile are used in place of bread.

What Can You Do?

Is there a custom in your family that has been passed down through the generations? Talk about some of the unique customs and traditions in your family and how they got started, if you know. Is there a favorite family recipe that your great-grandmother created because of an abundance of an ingredient in her homeland? Maybe there is a custom in your family that resulted from governmental persecution. Give thanks to God for ancestors who persevered and determinedly passed the stories of their generation on to the next.

What Does the Bible Say?

"Whether we live or die, it must be for God. . . . Alive or dead, we still belong to the Lord" (Romans 14:7–8).

Columbia ....

Buñuelos Antioquenos (Cheese Ball)

¼ cup cornstarch
2 cups cream cheese
1 teaspoon brown sugar
¼ teaspoon salt

½ teaspoon baking powder
1 egg yolk
¼ cup milk
Vegetable oil

Mix together the cornstarch, cheese, brown sugar, salt, and baking powder. Add the egg yolk and milk and beat well. Form into small balls and fry in deep vegetable oil.

Did You Know?

In 1971, Paolo Lugari decided to build a village on previously uninhabitable land in the South American country of Colombia. Not wanting to destroy the Colombian Amazon, or the El Choco rain forest, Lugari claimed 25,000 acres of Colombian grasslands. This area of barren soil is now the village of Gaviotas, Colombia. This village of 200 inhabitants has solar water-heating systems, community housing developments, and a hospital cooled by the wind and heated by the sun. Thousands of large windmills provide electricity for the residents. The city has no police department, jail, guns, or dogs. Citizens who break the community code are banished.

What Can You Do?

Gaviotas, Colombia, sounds almost perfect! Encourage each family member to draw his or her own perfect place to live. Be creative and inventive! Just as Gaviotas has planned for every need in its community, envision the systems that will be needed to provide food, water, electricity, and housing for your imaginary place. Then read together Genesis 1 from the Bible. God's perfect creation provided everything Adam and Eve needed. Discuss God's perfect plan and how humans help and hinder God's perfect place to live.

What Does the Bible Say?

"I think about the heavens. I think about what your fingers have created. I think about the moon and stars that you have set in place. What is a human being that you think about him? What is a son of man that you take care of him? You made him a little lower than the heavenly beings. You placed on him a crown of glory and honor" (Psalm 8:3–5 NIrV).

Empanadas (Meat Pies)

1 tablespoon butter	1 hard-boiled egg, chopped
⅓ cup chopped onion	½ cup cooked rice
½ cup chopped tomatoes	¾ teaspoon salt
½ pound lean ground beef	Pastry for double-crust pie, pur-
⅛ teaspoon pepper	chased
¼ teaspoon cumin	

Melt butter in skillet. Add onion and tomatoes and cook over low heat until onion is soft. Stir in beef and cook until no pink remains. Remove from heat and stir in remaining ingredients. Cool mixture. Roll out pastry; cut in 4-inch rounds. Place 1 tablespoon of filling in the center of each round. Brush edges with water and fold dough, pressing edges together firmly. Cut steam vent in top of each pie. Place pies on a slightly greased cookie sheet and bake in hot oven at 425°F until browned.

Did You Know?

Prized emeralds have been mined in Colombia for thousands of years. In fact, treasure hunters, known as quaqueros, still tunnel into the hillsides next to mines, risking suffocation and cave-ins to search for emeralds to illegally sell. Treasure hunting is a dangerous occupation. If caught by the national police, the quaqueros are put in jail. More dangerous than jail, though, are other quaqueros who are hunting for those same precious emeralds.

What Can You Do?

Create your own Colombian piñata from a large paper grocery bag. Decorate the outside of the bag using markers or crayons. Purchase individually wrapped candy and place inside the bag. Tie the top of the bag piñata closed with a 4-foot piece of twine, jute, or rope. Attach to the end of a broom handle. Blindfold one family member at a time and have each person try to hit the piñata with a plastic toy bat while Mom or Dad holds the piñata in the air. When the piñata is broken, the candy will spill out. After everyone gathers up the candy, sit down and have family members each give their candy to another. Discuss Proverbs 11:24 and the feelings each family member had as he or she generously gave his or her candy to another. Was this task a little more difficult for some?

What Does the Bible Say?

"Sometimes you can become rich by being generous or poor by being greedy" (Proverbs 11:24 CEV).

Costa Rica ....

Arroz con Leche (Rice Pudding)

2 cups rice
1 can sweetened condensed milk
1 can evaporated milk

2 cinnamon sticks
2 whole cloves
3 cups water

Cook rice in salted water until tender. Add remaining ingredients and mix with a fork. Simmer for 15 minutes. Serve warm.

Did You Know?

Coffee has been grown in Costa Rica since 1779. The perfect soil and climate make Costa Rica well suited for the coffee industry. When ripe, the hand-picked coffee beans are trucked to processing plants where they are washed to remove the outside layer of the bean. Then the moist beans dry in the sun until the leathery outer skin is able to be rubbed off by special machines. The beans are then vacuum-sealed and shipped around the world.

What Can You Do?

After Mom has had her cup of morning coffee, ask her to remove the coffee grounds and dry them on a paper towel to use for a family activity later in the evening. After dinner, mix together the 1 cup used, dry coffee grounds, ¼ cup salt, and ¾ cup cornmeal. Add just enough warm water to moisten the dry ingredients. (This dough should not stain because the cornmeal absorbs any remaining coffee coloring.) Spend time together creating coffee scented clay pots, coiled snakes, or maybe even a dough representation of the coastline of Costa Rica!

What Does the Bible Say?

"Yet, O Lord, you are our Father. We are the clay, you are the potter; we are all the work of your hand" (Isaiah 64:8 NIV).

Guatemala........

Turned-over Black Beans

2 pounds black beans
1 red onion, sliced
¼ cup oil
1 teaspoon salt

1 teaspoon minced garlic
1 teaspoon salt
½ teaspoon white pepper

Soak beans for 5 hours in water. Drain that water and place beans in clean water to cook. Keep beans just covered with water. Cook 1½ hours. When cooked, blend in a blender. Cook onion in oil until soft. Add the beans and other spices. Cook the beans over low heat until they can be turned over. Remove from pan and mold into a round shape on a plate. Serve as a dip with chips.

Did You Know?

Tikal National Park is the home to Guatemala's most impressive Mayan ruins. With over 4,000 structures, Tikal was inhabited from 800 B.C. to A.D. 900. The remains of Tikal indicate that it contained homes, businesses, ball courts, tombs of Mayan leaders, and numerous temples built for their gods. Hieroglyphic writings on the stone walls show images of a jaguar priest and a Mayan god that looks like a double-headed serpent. There are many theories as to why the Tikal site was abandoned in A.D. 900, however, no one really knows for sure why this civilization disbanded.

What Can You Do?

If a guest were to enter the door of your church, how would he know that members of your congregation believe in Jesus? And, if that guest were to attend the service, which portions of the service indicate that Christians are worshipping there? After attending church services this week, return to the sanctuary as a family to discuss some of the prominent Christian symbols displayed in the sanctuary. Encourage youngest family members to look for and count the number of crosses they see. Search for other visible symbols of Christ.

What Does the Bible Say?

"And this is the way to have eternal life—to know you, the only true God, and Jesus Christ, the one you sent to earth" (John 17:3 NLT).

Haiti ....

Baked Pineapple

3 eggs, separated
¾ cup sugar
1 large can crushed pineapple

1 cup bread crumbs
1 cup almonds

Blend egg yolks and sugar. Stir in pineapple and bread cubes. In a separate bowl, beat egg whites until stiff. Fold into mixture. Add almonds. Pour into a buttered casserole dish. Bake 40 minutes at 350°F.

Did You Know?

Do you have a need to get dirt under your fingernails and feel sweat dripping off your brow? Think agrotourism in Haiti! Agrotourism is similar to ecotourism; however, agrotourism focuses on agriculture. If you take an agrotour in Haiti, a Haitian farmer will guide you through a pineapple farm or sugarcane field and allow you to observe the growing, harvesting, and processing of the crop. And, many agrotourism packages include an overnight stay in the home of a local farmer and his family. Agrotourism benefits everyone involved. It provides funds for the Haitian farmers as an additional means of support for their families, and it enlightens the tourists to a country and lifestyle much different from their own.

What Can You Do?

As a family, take a walk through the park, a hike in the mountains, a swim in the ocean, or a rest under a tree. Have you ever stopped to trace the path of a roly-poly or counted the number of flowers a bee visits before flying away? Have you counted how many steps it takes to walk around the block? Have you scampered through the grass like a squirrel? Take a notepad and some pencils with you when you go. Write your observations for discussion later, or draw what you see while you are enjoying the view. Take a moment to thank God for His creation including His most intricate design—YOU!

What Does the Bible Say?

"All of God's creation and all that he rules, come and praise your Lord! With all my heart I praise the Lord!" (Psalm 103:22 CEV).

Honduras.........

Caribbean Rice

2 cups hot, cooked rice
11 ounces canned mandarin oranges, drained and coarsely chopped
8 ounces canned crushed pineapple, drained
½ cup chopped red pepper

½ cup slivered almonds, toasted
½ cup unsweetened grated coconut, toasted*
⅓ cup green onions, sliced
2 tablespoons mango chutney
¼ teaspoon ground ginger

Combine all ingredients in a large skillet. Cook and stir over medium-high heat until ingredients are blended and thoroughly heated.

***Note:** To toast coconut, spread grated coconut on an ungreased baking sheet and toast at 300°F for 1 minute.

Did You Know?

Mango chutney like that used in the Caribbean rice contains green, unripened mangos. In some countries, unripe mangos are served with salt or a salty condiment. However, in the US, many people prefer to eat raw mangoes when they are soft and juicy. Sweet, ripe mangoes are rich in vitamins A, B, and C. And, one more valuable use for mangoes—just one squirt of juice from a ripe mango can give immediate relief when applied to a scorpion bite or bee sting. When you are picking out mangoes at the grocery story, skip on by the over-ripe mangoes. They are said to taste like turpentine!

What Can You Do?

Are you sweet or sour? Do your words sting like turpentine? Genuine compliments should be sincere and not contrived. You need to practice what you say before your words can become a reliably sweet habit. How many sweet and juicy responses or compliments can you give to family members and friends today? Keep track of the kind responses and compliments you give today. At the end of the day, think back over your conversations. Are you surprised that your sweet responses and compliments rubbed off on others?

What Does the Bible Say?

"Kind words are like honey—sweet to the soul and healthy for the body" (Proverbs 16:24 NLT).

Paraguay ....

Rice Guiso

I tablespoon oil
Pork or beef (¼ to ½ pound)
I onion, chopped
I cup rice
I teaspoon salt

⅛ teaspoon pepper
I 3/4 cups water
2 tablespoons tomato paste
(optional)

Cut pork or beef into small cubes. Heat oil in heavy skillet, and brown meat well. Add onion, rice, salt, and pepper. Sauté briefly. Add water and tomato paste. Cover. Simmer about 30 minutes or until rice is tender.

Did You Know?

From 1864 to 1870, the Paraguayan people were involved in Paraguay's deadliest war. The Paraguayan War is also known as the War of the Triple Alliance because Paraguay fought with the triple alliance countries of Argentina, Brazil, and Uruguay. Paraguay was a country led by a dictator hungry for more territory and more power; however, it was no match for the power of these three countries. The war devastated the population, leaving only 221,000 of Paraguay's 525,000 people alive. Of the 221,000, only 28,000 were men.

What Can You Do?

War dominates our world. Between nations and people groups, the wars that we read about in newspapers can be on the same scale as the Paraguayan War, and even larger. But have you thought about the small battles that are going on every day in homes and neighborhoods near you? Is there a not-so-neighborly dispute over property lines or barking dogs in your community? Have there been hostilities at local footballs games or a youth hockey game? What about your friends and their families? Do you know of brothers and sisters who have bitter arguments or parents and teenagers who are experiencing a clash of wills? Today, in your family's own small way, try to practice peaceful cooperation and communication. When you are tempted to speak out against someone today, hold your tongue. Peacefully remember Proverbs 12:20 instead.

What Does the Bible Say?

"Deceit fills hearts that are plotting evil; joy fills hearts that are planning peace!" (Proverbs 12:20 NLT).

So'o-Yosopy (Beef Soup)

2 tablespoons vegetable oil
2 medium onions, finely
  chopped
1 green bell pepper, seeded
  and chopped
4 medium tomatoes, peeled
  and chopped

2 pounds ground lean sirloin
8 cups cold water
½ cup cooked rice or vermicelli
Salt
Grated Parmesan cheese

In a skillet, heat the oil and sauté the onions and peppers until onions are tender. Stir in tomatoes and cook about 5 minutes longer. Let the mixture cool slightly. Put the beef into another saucepan. Stir in the onions, pepper, and tomatoes (known as the sofrito). Add 8 cups cold water. Mix well. Bring to a boil over medium heat, stirring with a wooden spoon. Add the rice and simmer, still stirring, until tender (about 15 minutes). Add salt to taste. After pouring into serving bowls, sprinkle with Parmesan cheese.

Did You Know?

Paraguay lies in the central portion of South America, divided by the Paraguay River. Guarani, the language spoken by the first inhabitants of Paraguay, is still the language spoken at home by most Paraguayans. Spanish, however, is spoken in business, schools, and government. Guarani is also the name of Paraguay's money and Guarania is the style of music from Paraguay. The people of Paraguay eat many grains, such as maize (corn) and *manioc* (cassava). *Mate* (tea) and *mosto* (sugarcane juice) are the most common beverages.

What Can You Do?

Paraguay is a country of contrasts . . . wet and dry climates, rich and poor residents, urban and rural living. Fold a piece of paper in half. On one half of the paper, write down ten blessings in your life. On the opposite side of the paper, write how your life would be different without each of those ten blessings. Thank God for your blessings.

What Does the Bible Say?

"The Lord will bless you with rain at planting time. There will be wonderful harvests and plenty of pastureland for your cattle" (Isaiah 30:23 NLT).

Peru . . . .

Papas a La Huancaina (Potato Salad)

Boiled potatoes cut in half
10 ripe Greek olives
5 hard-boiled eggs
1 hot pepper, cut in strips

Sauce:
2 cups white goat cheese (or
other fresh cheese such as
feta)

3 hard-boiled egg yolks
Salt and pepper
2 tablespoons ground hot
pepper
1 cup oil
Several drops of lemon juice
½ cup evaporated milk
¼ cup onions, finely chopped

In a blender, mix cheese, egg yolks, salt, pepper, and ground hot pepper. Add oil gradually; then lemon juice, milk, and onions. Arrange potato halves on a serving plate. Cover potatoes with sauce; garnish with olives, quartered boiled eggs, and hot pepper strips. Prepare on a bed of lettuce on individual serving plates.

Did You Know?

Lake Titicaca, on the border between Peru and Bolivia, is the second largest lake in South America. In the middle of Lake Titicaca are the Uros Islands. These floating islands are formed from layers of totora reeds, which grow in shallow sections of the lake. Approximately 300 Uros people maintain the islands by continually harvesting and adding fresh totora reeds to the top as old reeds rot away from the bottom.

What Can You Do?

Try this experiment to learn about the properties of sound. Obtain a wide blade of grass with no tears or holes, about the length of your index finger. Hold your left hand up in front of you. Make a loose fist with your thumb pointing upward and your thumbnail toward you. With your right hand, put the blade of grass along the right side of your thumb. Bring your right thumb up beside your left, trapping the grass between your thumbs. Be sure the grass is stretched tightly across the gap between the first and second joints of your thumb. Now, put your thumbs to your mouth so that the gap is against your lips and blow hard.

What Does the Bible Say?

"But when she could hide him no longer, she got a papyrus basket for him and coated it with tar and pitch. Then she placed the child in it and put it among the reeds along the bank of the Nile. His sister stood at a distance to see what would happen to him" (Exodus 2:3–4 NIV).

Venezuela ....

Guacamole

2 ripe avocados
½ onion
1 large ripe tomato
2 teaspoons salt

Dash of pepper
2 tablespoons Worcestershire sauce
½ teaspoon lemon juice

Peel and mash avocados. Place mashed avocados, onion, and tomato in a blender or food processor Blend until smooth. Add salt, pepper, Worcestershire sauce, and lemon juice. Blend again until smooth.

Did You Know?

Avocados are healthy. Although they are high in fat, the fat is unsaturated—the good kind. They are packed with vitamins A, C, and E and are very high in protein and dietary fiber. Avocado trees can grow up to 80 feet high and live for many years. The tree serves as a warehouse. Since the fruit does not ripen until it is picked, it can stay on the tree for several months.

What Can You Do?

For your next family project, grow an avocado tree! Wash and dry a pit from one of the avocados used to make the guacamole. Find the circumference of the pit, and insert three toothpicks equal distance around the pit with the pointed end of the pit facing downward. Fill a glass or jar with lukewarm water and balance the pit, wide end down, over the top of the jar so that the base of the pit is below the waterline. Make sure this end is always under water. Keep the pit out of direct sunlight and wait two to six weeks for the roots to emerge. You may then plant the entire avocado pit and sprout in a container filled with potting soil. Be sure to place your avocado plant in a sunny indoor location, and water it regularly.

What Does the Bible Say?

"The fruit that godly people bear is like a tree of life. And those who lead others to do what is right are wise" (Proverbs 11:30 NIrV).

Stirring Up a World of Fun in

a World of Fun in

WESTERN EUROPE

Austria	Great Britain	Scotland
Belgium	Italy	Spain
France	Portugal	

Austria . . . .

Goulash

1 tablespoon vinegar
3 white onions, sliced
⅓ cup pork fat (shortening and a small amount of bacon can be substituted)
½ to ¾ pound sweet red or yellow peppers, diced

2 pounds pork, cubed
1 teaspoon salt
1 teaspoon caraway seeds
2 cloves garlic, pressed
½ to ¾ teaspoon marjoram
¼ cup water

Dilute vinegar with water and set aside. Sauté onions in hot fat until golden. Add peppers; stir very briefly (otherwise the peppers will turn bitter). Add vinegar-water mixture. Steam briefly, then add meat, salt, caraway seeds, garlic, and marjoram. Cover loosely and steam in its own juices, allowing juices to reduce several times, adding a small amount of water each time. (This is the only way to retain the brown juice of Viennese goulash.) When the meat is tender, add water to cover the meat. Simmer gently for another 15 minutes until some of the fat rises to the surface.

Did You Know?

Wolfgang Amadeus Mozart was born in Salzburg, Austria, in 1756. He was christened with the name Johannes Chrysostomus Wolfgangus Theophilus Mozart. However, Mozart changed portions of his name several times throughout his life before finally settling on Wolfgang Amadeus Mozart. The son of a composer and violin teacher, Mozart learned to play the violin as a toddler. As a young child, he was even able to play the violin blindfolded.

What Can You Do?

Before eating dinner, turn on a radio or stereo for some mood music during the meal. During dinner, talk about different kinds of music you heard today. Did you sing worship songs during a church service? Did you hear your favorite song on the radio? Maybe you heard a family member playing his or her musical instrument today. Talk about how favorite songs evoke special feelings and emotions. If available, listen to a segment of a Wolfgang Amadeus Mozart composition. After listening, discuss the mood and style of the piece. Thank God for the gift of music, which adds richness to life.

What Does the Bible Say?

"Sing a new song to the LORD! Let the whole earth sing to the LORD!" (Psalm 96:1 NLT).

Belgium ....

Boter Wafels (Butter Waffles)

4 cups milk	8⅓ cups flour
1 pound butter (no substitutes)	2 tablespoons baking powder
	2 teaspoons vanilla
4 cups fine sugar	4 eggs

Warm milk and butter in a saucepan until the butter melts. Add sugar. Sift flour and baking powder together and add to the mixture along with the vanilla and finally the eggs. Drop 2 tablespoons of dough onto the hot waffle iron. Makes approximately 70 waffles/cookies.

Did You Know?

Butter is a food fit for angels. In fact, Sarah and Abraham, of Old Testament fame, served cool milk and butter to three visiting angels. The word butter means "cow cheese" in Greek; however, it can be made from sheep, goat, or camel milk. People in Abraham and Sarah's day may have made butter in an animal skin container with a small opening at the bottom. This skin could be hung on poles and swung back and forth to churn the butter. Churning butter in an animal-skin container or in a more modern potter jar is a time-consuming task because it takes 21 pounds of cow's milk to make 1 pound of butter.

What Can You Do?

Before sitting down for dinner, work together as a family to make your own fresh butter. Pour 1/2 cup (room-temperature) thick whipping cream into a glass jar with a tight-fitting lid. Take turns shaking the jar until a lump of butter forms. It will take about 10 to 15 minutes. You might want to read the story of Abraham and Sarah and their angelic visitors in Genesis 18 while you take turns shaking the jar. When the lump of butter has formed, open the jar and pour off the thin liquid. Thank God for His provisions, then spread the butter son a warm piece of bread.

What Does the Bible Say?

"The Lord appeared to Abraham near the large trees of Mamre. Abraham was sitting at the entrance to his tent. It was the hottest time of the day. Abraham looked up and saw three men standing nearby. He quickly left the entrance to his tent to meet them. He bowed low to the ground. . . . Then he brought some butter and milk and the calf that had been prepared. He served them to the three men" (Genesis 18:1–2, 8 NIrV).

France ....

Buche de Noel (Yule Log Cake)

4 eggs
½ teaspoon salt
¾ cup sugar
I teaspoon vanilla extract
¾ cup packaged pancake mix
I cup powdered sugar

Chocolate filling:
I (4-serving size) package
   instant chocolate pudding mix
2 (1¼-ounce) envelopes Dream
   Whip®
1¼ cups cold milk

Place eggs and salt in blender container. Cover; blend until frothy. Add sugar and vanilla; cover; blend 30 to 60 seconds or until smooth. Add pancake mix; cover; blend for 20 seconds or until combined. Pour batter into greased and floured 15-by-10-by-1-inch jelly-roll pan. Bake in a 400°F oven for 8 to 10 minutes. Loosen sides; turn cake out onto towel sprinkled with powdered sugar. Starting with long edge, roll up cake in towel. Cool. Combine all ingredients for chocolate filling. Beat at medium speed of electric mixer for 2 to 3 minutes or until fluffy. Unroll cake; spread with ½ of the chocolate filling. Reroll cake. Frost the cake with the remaining filling. The cake should resemble a log. Using a fork, run the tines the length of the log to simulate bark. Chill. Just before serving, sift powdered sugar over the log, to simulate snow. Slice crosswise to serve.

Did You Know?

During the Middle Ages, the burning of the Yule log became a winter family tradition. The oldest and the youngest members of a family would carry a decorated log to the fireplace where it burned throughout the night. The ashes collected the next morning were thought to protect the home and its residents from natural disasters, illnesses, and the devil. Buche de noel became the French dessert served for Christmas dinner in 1879.

What Can You Do?

Begin an anytime-of-year tradition by making a Yule log cake and creating a prayer log. While eating your Yule log cake, encourage family members to write short prayers on small sticky notes. Then as you pray for each item listed, attach these notes to a piece of log or a tree limb. Keep the prayer log in a prominent place throughout the year, returning to it frequently to pray for items listed. When a prayer is answered, remove the sticky note from the log, and add new prayers as needed. At the end of a year, burn the log, giving prayers completely to Jesus.

What Does the Bible Say?

"The prayer of an innocent person is powerful, and it can help a lot" (James 5:16 CEV).

Crepes

1 cup flour	1 large egg
1 tablespoon sugar, optional (for a dessert crepe)	1 tablespoon melted butter
1 cup milk	Fruit or jam

Combine flour and sugar. Then add milk and egg and beat until smooth. Add butter and mix lightly. Batter should be the consistency of thick cream. Add milk if it is too thick. Butter an 8-inch nonstick skillet and heat until butter is hot but not burned. Ladle ¼ cup of batter into the hot pan and rotate the pan to cover the entire surface with batter. Cook the crepe until it is slightly brown on the edges and dry on top. Turn the crepe over with a spatula and continue to cook it for about 20 seconds. Remove the crepe from the pan. Grease the pan between every 1 or 2 crepes. Repeat cooking until all the batter is gone. Place filling on each crepe and roll it up. Use fruit or jam as filling and topping. Or try it with lemon juice and a sprinkle of sugar. For a meal, fill the crepes with meat, vegetables, or cheese.

Did You Know?

The Tour de France bicycle race pedaled into history in 1903. It is a 21-day race that covers more than 2,000 miles throughout the countryside of France. Bicyclers pedal an average of 324,000 times, wear out about 3 bicycle chains, and use an average of 792 bicycle tires throughout the course of the race. Each competitor burns an average of 5,900 calories per day for a total of 123,900 calories over the 21-day trek.

What Can You Do?

Create your own Tour de Denver, Tour de Pine Street, or Tour de East Longmont family bike race. As a family, plan your course (safely away from traffic) and set a date. Make sure everyone has appropriate protective gear, and encourage each bicycler to decorate his or her bike with crepe paper streamers attached to the handlebars or to create "Tour de" license plates or signs. Invite friends and neighbors to join in, if you wish. Those who can't bike can be the fans who stand on the side of the street and cheer the competitors to victory. Remind everyone that the goal of the family race is not winning with the fastest time, but enjoying the healthy exercise and time together as a family. Begin the bike race with prayer for a safe and enjoyable race.

What Does the Bible Say?

"Physical exercise has some value, but spiritual exercise is much more important, for it promises a reward in both this life and the next" (1 Timothy 4:8 NLT).

Flan aux Poire (Pear Flan)

2 large pears
2 tablespoons sugar
⅓ cup butter
2 eggs

¾ cup milk
¾ cup whipping cream
4 pinches of cinnamon

Peel the pears and cut them in half. Remove the seeds; then slice the pears. Put the sliced pears in a saucepan with 2 tablespoons of sugar. Cook over a low heat until the pears are tender. Preheat the oven at 300°F. Using butter, grease ovenproof individual serving bowls. In a mixing bowl, stir eggs, milk, whipping cream, and cinnamon. Pour this mixture into individual serving bowls and top with pear slices. Bake for 1 hour. Serve warm. You may want to add chocolate sauce before serving.

Did You Know?

The pear, a relative to the apple, became popular in France during the seventeenth century when King Louis XIV proclaimed the pear his favorite fruit. Even today, fresh fruit is one of the most popular French desserts. Recent studies have found that French women eat far more fresh fruit, including pears, than women in the United States. Healthier eating habits, smaller portion sizes, and increased exercise cause researchers to believe that French women are healthier than women in the US. OK, so maybe just take a small portion of flan aux poire!

What Can You Do?

Have family members keep track of each morsel of food that passes their lips today. Yes, even count those three chocolate-covered peanuts you found at the bottom of your backpack. Search the Internet for the caloric and nutritional content of each food you ate and see if each item fits into a healthy eating lifestyle. Some useful sites, as well as others you might find, are: http://www.lifeclinic.com/focus/nutrition/food-pyramid.asp, or http://www.ring.com/health/food/food.htm.

What Does the Bible Say?

"You realize, don't you, that you are the temple of God, and God himself is present in you? No one will get by with vandalizing God's temple, you can be sure of that. God's temple is sacred—and you, remember, are the temple" (1 Corinthians 3:16–17 The Message).

Great Britain........

Cucumber Sandwiches

Bread   **Cucumber**
Cream cheese

Trim crusts from bread. Spread softened cream cheese on half of the bread slices. Put thinly sliced pieces of peeled cucumber on the other half of the bread slices. Put one cream cheese bread slice and one cucumber bread slice together and cut into fourths. Serve with hot tea mixed with sugar and milk, or fruit juice.

Did You Know?

"Cool as a cucumber" is more than just a saying referring to someone who is calm and relaxed under pressure. The inside temperature of a cucumber is up to 20°F cooler than the temperature outside its skin. Cucumbers, which are 95 percent water, are the cool relatives of pumpkins, zucchini, and watermelons. You might want to keep your cool if you are allergic to pollen or aspirin; cucumbers could cause your mouth to itch. On the other hand, cucumbers are used to help treat arthritis, gout, and other maladies!

What Can You Do?

Invite neighborhood friends to a special afternoon tea. Or, prepare tea for parents and grandparents. With Mom's permission, get out the fancy tablecloth, special plates, cups, and silverware. Begin by serving several kinds of tea followed by homemade cucumber sandwiches, fresh berries with whipped cream, and scones. Pray for the world and, just for fun, learn to say the word *cucumber* in five different languages.

le concombre (French)
die gurke (German)
il cetriolo (Italian)
el pepino (Spanish)
gurka (Swedish)

What Does the Bible Say?

"The riff-raff among the people had a craving and soon they had the People of Israel whining, 'Why can't we have meat? We ate fish in Egypt—and got it free!—to say nothing of the cucumbers and melons, the leeks and onions and garlic. But nothing tastes good out here; all we get is manna, manna, manna'" (Numbers 11:4–6 The Message).

Fish and Chips

Fish sticks
Fried potatoes (frozen French fries)

Newspaper
Salt
Malt vinegar (if desired)

Prepare fish sticks and fried potatoes as directed on the packages. Wrap a serving of fish and potatoes (chips) in a small piece of newspaper made into a cone. Season with salt and malt vinegar.

Did You Know?

Try having a staring contest with a fish! The fact is you'll always lose. Fish don't blink. Fish are not capable of blinking because they have no eyelids. Actually, fish don't need to blink. The purpose of blinking is to spread moisture from the tear ducts over the surface of the eyes. Since fish live in water, the surface of the eye is always wet!

What Can You Do?

Set out some art supplies such as colored pencils, markers, paper, crayons, or watercolor paints, and paper. After dinner, draw a portrait of another family member's eye. Remember, each person's artwork is unique and creative. Don't worry about getting every last detail correct. Surely a picture of Mom's eye, Picasso-style, is suitable for framing on the kitchen refrigerator.

What Does the Bible Say?

"Let us fix our eyes on Jesus, the author and perfecter of our faith, who for the joy set before him endured the cross, scorning its shame, and sat down at the right hand of the throne of God" (Hebrews 12:2 NIV).

Scottish Shortbread

4½ cups flour
1 pound butter

1 cup sugar
1 teaspoon vanilla

Mix all ingredients together until they form a ball of dough. Divide dough into 2 rolls, 2 inches wide. Chill overnight. Slice rolls into ½-inch slices and bake at 350°F for about 20 minutes until golden.

Did You Know?

James M. Barrie, an early twentieth century Scottish playwright and novelist, could never quite live up to his mother's expectations. Even after the death of his older brother, who was his mother's favorite son, James continued to be a disappointment in her eyes. As an adult, James only grew to be five feet one, which continually caused him to be mistaken for a young boy. James's childhood and small size became the basis for his writing of the well-loved story about a boy who never grew up, Peter Pan.

What Can You Do?

Create a growth chart for each child in the family by taping several pieces of paper together, end to end, or using a strip of paper from a roll of newsprint or butcher paper. After each child has had the opportunity to decorate and personalize his or her growth chart, place the chart in a location where it may remain for several months or years. Upon measuring each child, and recording the height and date on the chart, Mom or Dad should also write a personal, positive comment about each child's personality or a short story about the child at the current height and weight. Take measurements often and write positive comments frequently!

What Does the Bible Say?

"So Jesus grew both in height and in wisdom, and he was loved by God and by all who knew him" (Luke 2:52 NLT).

Trifle

I prepared angel food cake
Strawberry jam
Custard or vanilla pudding (pre-
    pared according to manufac-
    turer's instructions)

Whipped topping
Almonds

In a trifle dish, layer in order: cake, jam, custard or vanilla pudding, whipped topping, and almonds. Serve immediately.

Did You Know?

The members of All Saints' Church in Terling, England, have found a creative way of fund-raising by hosting an International Trifle Festival each year. Church members use recipes from England, Wales, Australia, France, and other points around the world for judges to critique and villagers to pay to taste. One unique entry was a breakfast trifle made with bacon and eggs; and a Sunday roast beef trifle has been suggested.

What Can You Do?

Does your church or a local service agency have an ongoing need for certain items? Maybe your church's education programs are always in need of glue, construction paper, markers, and tape. Maybe the local animal shelter always has a need for donations of dog or cat food. As a family, work together to host a bake sale to raise money to purchase these needed supplies. Designate an entire Saturday for baking, packaging, and pricing. Freeze the food items and host the bake sale the following Saturday or Sunday in your neighborhood, or even at church, after receiving permission.

What Does the Bible Say?

"Generosity begets generosity. Stinginess impoverishes" (Mark 4:25 The Message).

Italy ■ ■ ■ ■ ■ ■ ■ ■

Braciolette a Forno (Baked Pork Chops)

¼ cup butter
I ounce dried mushrooms
I tablespoon flour
I cup broth
I teaspoon tomato paste
I bouillon cube
I egg

3 tablespoons parsley, chopped
Salt and pepper
4 large pork chops
I large carrot
I small onion
I stalk celery

Melt 2 tablespoons butter in heavy skillet. Add soaked and drained mushrooms. Brown them. Add flour, broth, tomato paste, and a bouillon cube. Reserve this sauce. Beat the egg; add chopped parsley, salt, and pepper. Dip the pork chops in the egg mixture and fry in the rest of butter with I tablespoon oil. Brown them on both sides. Place in casserole dish. Add finely chopped carrot, onion, and celery. Add mushroom sauce. Bake in oven at 375°F for 30 to 40 minutes.

Did You Know?

While eating your braciolette a forno with pasta, wow your guests with these snippets of Italian trivia. Italy is about the size of Arizona. Inventions that have come from Italy are: the thermometer, the piano, the ice-cream cone, eyeglasses, and pizza, of course! The average Italian eats 55 pounds of pasta in a year. That's 165 cups of pasta! And if you are counting calories, 165 cups of pasta, without any of those yummy Italian sauces or even without any braciolette a forno, comes to 28,050 calories!

What Can You Do?

Set a few pasta noodles aside before eating dinner tonight. After dinner, provide each family member with a piece of white construction paper, thin tempera or acrylic paints, and a couple of pasta noodles. Encourage each member of the family to create an artistic masterpiece, using the pasta as a paintbrush. After these works of art are complete, have family members try to interpret the paintings of others before the artist discusses his or her work. When finished, find a perfect location to display the pasta paintings for a week or two, remembering to compliment the artist each time you pass by his or her painting.

What Does the Bible Say?

"For we are God's masterpiece. He has created us anew in Christ Jesus, so that we can do the good things he planned for us long ago" (Ephesians 2:10 NLT).

Portugal.........

Portuguese Delight

1 can condensed milk
1 can whole milk (fill the
  empty can with whole milk)
1½ tablespoons cornstarch
4 egg yolks
4 egg whites

¼ cup sugar
1 teaspoon vanilla extract
12 ounces chocolate chips
Graham crackers
1 medium container whipped
  topping

Mix condensed milk, 1 can of whole milk, and cornstarch in a saucepan and cook over low heat, stirring constantly until mixture begins to boil. Boil 3 minutes and remove from heat. In a separate mixing bowl, beat egg yolks and slowly add hot mixture, stirring constantly. Return to low heat and boil for 3 minutes, stirring constantly. Remove from heat and allow to cool completely (perhaps for 2 hours). Beat egg whites into peaks, adding sugar and vanilla. Fold into cooled pudding mixture. Melt chocolate chips. Cover the bottom of an 8-by-8 casserole dish with graham crackers and pour melted chocolate chips on top. Allow to cool 5 minutes. Pour pudding mixture over top of graham crackers and top with whipped topping. Sprinkle with shavings of a chocolate bar if desired.

Did You Know?

Portuguese black pottery, now handcrafted by fewer than one dozen potters, has been a tradition in Molelos, Portugal, for thousands of years. Pots are created on a wheel and smoothed with small stones that are often passed down from father to son for generations, sometimes over 150 years. These stones create distinctive patterns unique to each family of potters. The clay pieces then go into a kiln to slowly bake with pine bark and branches to create the deep, silvery, black color that Portuguese black pottery is known for.

What Can You Do?

As a family, go for a walk in the neighborhood and have each family member select a small stone to bring home. When you arrive home, rinse the stones with water, noticing intricate details that may not previously have been seen. Isn't it amazing that God created stones with distinctively unique qualities? The Portuguese potters, who have special stones for their work, have realized this. Place each person's stone on his or her pillow as a reminder to thank God for the uniqueness of all His creation, especially the wonderful uniqueness of each family member.

What Does the Bible Say?

"Yet, O Lord, you are our Father. We are the clay, you are the potter; we are all the work of your hand" (Isaiah 64:8 NIV).

Scotland . . . .

Scottish Eggs

8 hard-boiled eggs, peeled
¼ cup plain flour
1 pound pork sausage
¾ cup dry bread crumbs

½ teaspoon ground sage
¼ teaspoon salt
2 eggs, beaten
Vegetable oil

Coat each egg with flour. Divide sausage into 8 parts. Pat 1 part onto each egg. Mix bread crumbs, sage, and salt. Dip sausage-coated eggs into beaten eggs. Roll in bread crumb mixture. Fry eggs in 1½ to 2 inches of oil for 5 to 6 minutes. Turn occasionally. Drain on paper towels. Serve hot or cold.

Did You Know?

It takes a hen about 24 to 26 hours to lay an egg. But her work is never done. After laying an egg, and resting about half an hour, her body can begin making another egg. Some hens decide to take a break from egg laying once in a while. Scientists are not quite sure why a hen decides to take a break. But, a hen can rest anywhere from three to ten days, depending on how industrious she is. All in all, if a hen lays an average of five eggs a week, 50 weeks of the year, she will lay about 250 eggs each year.

What Can You Do?

Save the eggshells from all 8 eggs when making Scottish eggs. Grind the eggshells into a fine powder using a blender or food processor. Mix 1 tablespoon of the eggshell powder, 1 teaspoon of very hot water, and 1 teaspoon of flour in a small paper cup. Let the chalk dry for several days in a warm location. When the chalk is dry, peel away the paper cup and use your chalk to make a family hopscotch game on the sidewalk.

What Does the Bible Say?

"Birds find nooks and crannies in your house, sparrows and swallows make nests there. They lay their eggs and raise their young, singing their songs in the place where we worship. . . . How blessed they are to live and sing there!" (Psalm 84:3–4 The Message).

Spain........

Churros

1 cup water	Vegetable oil, enough to be 1
½ cup margarine or butter	to 1½ inches deep in the pan
¼ teaspoon salt	¼ cup sugar
1 cup flour	¼ teaspoon cinnamon
3 eggs	

Heat water, margarine, and salt in a saucepan. When the mix begins to boil, slowly stir in flour. Stir until the mixture forms a ball. Remove from the heat. Beat the eggs well and add them into the saucepan. Place the mixture in a plastic bag and seal the bag. Cut off the tip of one bottom corner of the bag. Heat the oil in a frying pan. Squeeze strips of dough into the oil. Fry a few strips at a time for 2 minutes per side or until golden brown. Remove the churros from the oil and drain on a paper towel. Sprinkle with a mixture of sugar and cinnamon.

Did You Know?

Churros are a sweet fried snack popular in Spain, Mexico, Brazil, Argentina, and the United States. Even the country of Turkey has its own version of churros called *tulumba tatlisi.* Churros were invented by Spanish shepherds who named them after the shape of the horns of the churro breed of sheep. In Spain, churros are very popular, especially when street vendors fry and sell them hot from their carts. And, when you are in Spain, try your hot churro dipped in a special rich, hot chocolate drink. Yum!

What Can You Do?

Pay close attention to the dinner conversation some night. Place a piece of paper and a pencil on the table and write down each time a family member remembers sheep being mentioned in the Bible. When you are finished with the meal, look up some of the following Bible passages about sheep. Say a prayer of thanksgiving for Jesus, the Good Shepherd who watches over His sheep—us.

Leviticus 7:23	Song of Solomon 4:2
1 Samuel 16:18–20	Matthew 18:12–14
Psalm 100:2–4	John 10:11–12

What Does the Bible Say?

"You were lost sheep with no idea who you were or where you were going. Now you're named and kept for good by the Shepherd of your souls" (1 Peter 2:25 The Message).

Gazpacho (Chilled Vegetable Soup)

3 large tomatoes, peeled
1 large cucumber, peeled
1 green pepper
1 medium onion, peeled
¼ cup olive oil

1 cup tomato juice
2 tablespoons white vinegar
1 clove garlic
Salt and pepper to taste
Croutons

Chop the first four ingredients into small pieces and put them into the blender. Add the next 4 ingredients to the blender. Sprinkle in the salt and pepper. Put the cover on the blender and blend for 1 to 2 minutes. Chill. Serve the soup topped with croutons.

Did You Know?

The Agricultural Research Service has conducted a scientific study on the effects of eating 17 ounces of gazpacho every day for two weeks. Blood samples taken from 12 healthy people before and after the study indicate that eating vegetable-laden gazpacho helped reduce study participants' levels of stress molecules, an indicator of improved health. More research is in the works. These scientists are out to prove that Mother does know best! After all, hasn't she always told you to eat your vegetables?

What Can You Do?

As a family, plan the dinner menus for the week to come. Don't forget fruits and vegetables! When selecting favorite meals, include meals that family members can take turns preparing. (You may want to include several recipes from this book.) Create a shopping list and head for the grocery store as a family to purchase the supplies you will need for the coming week's dinners.

What Does the Bible Say?

"Better a meal of vegetables where there is love, than a fattened calf with hatred" (Proverbs 15:17 NIV).

Spanish Tortilla (Spanish Omelet)

6 to 7 medium-sized potatoes   **4 to 5 eggs**
⅓ cup olive oil   **½ teaspoon salt**

Peel and dice potatoes or cut them into thin slices. Heat oil in a skillet and add potatoes. Stir completely to coat each potato with oil. Reduce heat and keep stirring potatoes to avoid browning. Drain off oil after potatoes are soft. Put potatoes in a bowl. Beat together eggs and salt, stir in potatoes, and mix well. Return oil to pan and reheat. Pour in egg mixture. Let egg mixture set on the bottom of the pan, regulating heat so it doesn't burn. Use a spatula to firm edges. Shake the pan frequently to keep bottom of tortilla from sticking. Place a plate over the pan and flip the tortilla out of the pan onto the plate. Add more oil to the pan and slide tortilla back in to cook other side. Remove when it is golden brown.

Did You Know?

OK, if a stormy day has kept you inside and made you grumpy, think about the people who live in Spain. It has approximately 10,000 storms a year, and more than 60,000 bolts of lightning were recorded there on one day (August 17, 2003). The wettest village in Spain has an average of 84 inches of rain in a year. Some villages near the higher mountains in Spain have wind speeds up to 124 miles per hour. Spain has a wide range of temperatures also. In Estany Gento, the temperatures can be as low as -25°F, and in Ecija, also known as the frying pan of Andalucia, the temperature can be as warm as 116°F.

What Can You Do?

On a boring, rainy evening, create raindrop paintings. Sprinkle small amounts of several colors of powdered drink mix on pieces of thick white construction paper or cardstock. Put on your raincoats, forget about those umbrellas, and go outside to create a masterpiece. Carefully hold the paper seasoned with colorful drink mix flat in the rain. Watch the rain splash on the powdered drink mix, forming designs. Thank God for earth-quenching rain as you create raindrop paintings. Carry the paintings in the house and let dry flat before displaying them on the refrigerator! Your raindrop paintings will smell yummy too!

What Does the Bible Say?

"Yet He has not left himself without testimony: He has shown kindness by giving you rain from heaven and crops in their seasons; He provides you with plenty of food and fills your hearts with joy" (Acts 14:17 NIV).

Index ....

New Hope® Publishers is a division of WMU®,
an international organization that challenges Christian
believers to understand and be radically involved in
God's mission. For more information about WMU,
go to www.wmu.com. More information
about New Hope books may be found at
www.newhopepublishers.com. New Hope books
may be purchased at your local bookstore.